On the Wings of Self-Esteem

Gina —
You are a winner!
All my love,
Louise ♡♥

ON THE
WINGS OF
SELF-ESTEEM

A Companion for
Personal Transformation

by Louise Hart, Ed.D.

Celestial Arts
Berkeley, California

Celestial Arts
P.O. Box 7123
Berkeley, California 94707

Text design by Victor Ichioka
Cover design by 5th St. Design
Illustrated by Kristen Baumgardner Caven
FIRST CELESTIAL ARTS PRINTING 1994

Library of Congress Cataloging-in-Publication Data

Hart, Louise
     On the wings of self-esteem : a companion for personal
transformation / by Louise Hart.
        p.   cm.
     ISBN 0-89087-731-9
     1. Self-esteem. I. Title.
BF697.5.S46H36   1994
158'.1—dc20   94-14628
                                                                    CIP

Printed in the United States of America

1 2 3 4 5 / 98 97 96 95 94

On the day you were born

Your story passed from animal to animal:

The reindeer told the arctic terns

Who told the humpback whales

Who told the monarch butterflies

Who told the green turtles

Who told the European eel

Who told the busy garden warbler

And the marvelous news migrated around the world.

—Debra Frasier

· CONTENTS ·

PART III – WINGS OF SELF-ESTEEM

Acknowledgements

My loving, heartfelt gratitude to those who shared their insights, encouragement, stories, and wisdom, especially Dr. Patricia Palmer, Dr. Leah Subotnik, Dr. Ani Ligget, Ted and Diane Coffelt, and my son, Damian Baumgardner. Thanks also to Dave Caven, Joy, and others who contributed stories of their personal transformation.

Very special thanks to my daughter, friend, cheerleader, and editor, Kristen Baumgardner Caven who provided support every step of the way, even contributing the illustrations for this book.

And finally, much appreciation to David Hinds, Veronica Randall, and the capable staff at Celestial Arts.

INTRODUCTION

Y EARS AGO, a friend said to me, "Louise, it seems as though humans have a reverse metamorphosis. We start out as beautiful butterflies, then are turned into ugly caterpillars. We spend the rest of our lives trying to remember and become the beautiful creatures we once were." I have never forgotten those words.

When we were born we were innocent, truthful beings; we were trusting, open, and curious. Then, with the onset of harsh relationships, conflicts, and life experiences, we learned that it is not safe to be who we are. We adapted and adjusted to fit into the land of the giants who controlled every aspect of our existence. In this unsafe environment, we protected and defended ourselves by building a cocoon.

This book is based on the premise that self-esteem is the inborn, unconditional feeling of love, security, and well being that is crucial to our mental health. As we grow older, this positive force becomes buried under layers and layers of defense mechanisms. Yet self-esteem is our birthright. The purpose of *Wings* is to help recover and access the deep power and beauty that every human—and every one of God's creatures—possesses.

Healing yourself involves being willing to look at the holes, then filling the holes to become whole. It involves understanding what happened, letting go of past hurts and insecurities, and moving on to a better place. It is founded on compassion for yourself, affirming that you have always been okay—even when you felt like a lowly, plodding caterpillar. Recovering self-esteem is a journey in discovering the remnants of your self-worth, and sewing them together into your wings, the tapestry of your life.

In an archetypal hero's journey, according to Joseph Campbell, author of *Hero with a Thousand Faces*, there are three stages to spiritual empowerment: separation from the past, encounter with power, and the return to one's community to participate in a new way. Every significant human ritual includes these stages, each to symbolize a change in life status. And so with this book. *Wings* is organized in three parts to honor these stages.

The journey to mental, spiritual, and emotional health takes time. It involves stages of growth and stages of waiting. Because of the busyness of our lives, I have attempted to write *Wings* as a succinct seed packet of ideas that can germinate and grow within as you go about your daily life.

A journal can be a powerful companion on this journey. Take some quiet time to write when you need to listen to voices you don't usually hear. There are many ways to use a journal. You can use it as your best friend to share your insights and memories. You can record, as I have, the pits and peaks of the week. Use it as a tool to remember the child that you used to be; that child is still there, the butterfly that may have disguised itself as a caterpillar. Use it as your witness to observe your growth process on a day-to-day basis.

A butterfly begins its life as a crawling, wiggling caterpillar. As nature takes its course, the caterpillar metamorphoses into an elegant flying insect. The evolution to maturity is a natural and beautiful process. In *Wings* we will move through the cycle of transformation in the *right* direction—from caterpillar to butterfly. Part One describes childhood in a troubled family set in a society that teaches us to fear, hate, and harm ourselves. It ends with the willingness to leave the caterpillar life behind. Part Two is about spinning a "cocoon." It offers a series of exercises toward recovering self-esteem and empowering oneself. Finally, Part Three is about the completed transformation—being a butterfly, learning to fly, and living your life in a whole new way.

PART I

BUTTERFLIES
AND
CATERPILLARS

1

ON BECOMING A BUTTERFLY

The Process of Metamorphosis

"You must want to fly so much that you are willing to give up being a caterpillar."

—Trina Paulus, *Hope for the Flowers*

WHEN I WAS a new schoolteacher, the first graders brought in some large brown cocoons, which laid for many weeks gathering dust on the science table. One spring day, classroom activities screeched to a halt when one cocoon after another began to twitch and wiggle. By and by, each pod broke open and a newborn moth crept into the light. The creatures unfurled their limp wings into lovely tapestries. Day after day we witnessed this miracle of transformation. If a cocoon started rocking late in the day, I would take it home with me, even out to dinner, so I wouldn't miss its debut into the world.

The main biological purpose of butterflies and moths is to reproduce (as it is with all living beings). They do so by laying eggs that hatch as larvae, also known as caterpillars. A caterpillar's job in life (like all growing things) is to eat and grow and let go of layer after layer of its smaller self. Periodically, its body gets "too big for its britches" so it must shed its skin. The tight skin splits to reveal a new inner layer that will keep it together and protect it until the next stage. During its larval stage, a monarch butterfly sheds its zebra-striped skin four times, increasing in size and body weight some thirty times. Then, something changes. Guided by a mysterious instinct or inner wisdom, the caterpillar abruptly stops eating and enters its next phase.

I once observed this in a "pet" caterpillar that suddenly stopped eating and began to crawl around its cage tirelessly. My young doctor husband and I provided it with a branch that had three sturdy twigs. The caterpillar inspected it thoroughly and positioned itself at the juncture. Thread by thread, it began the lengthy, intense process of weaving a safe winter home. Holding tightly to the branch with its lower feet, it waved its upper body from side to side, fastening strands on one twig then another, hour after hour, until it was completely encapsulated in silk. Though this particular caterpillar had never before done this, it spun its cocoon like a pro. We would never see this little creature again in this form.

This particular caterpillar was a moth caterpillar; a butterfly caterpillar has a different way of doing things. When the time is right, it attaches its abdomen to the underside of a leaf. Then, with a series of spasms, it splits its outer skin and sheds one last coat. This innermost layer hardens into a sturdy armor, called a chrysalis, which serves as a cozy refuge for the growing insect during the long winter months.

To observers, nothing seems to be happening during the pupal stage. But this time of silence and withdrawal from the world is actually a period of intense creativity. The earthbound caterpillar is miraculously transforming itself into a winged creature of the sky. This extremely complex event happens in accord with nature, orchestrated by the butterfly's genetic code and the timing of the seasons.

Come springtime, after months enveloped in its insect womb, the life force quickens: "It's time!" The creature struggles to be born again, using all its strength to break out of its once cozy but now stifling cocoon or chrysalis. The adult's first appearance is disheveled and moist. Limp wings lay against its large body like a shawl. It contracts rhythmically, then rests. And again. With each pulse, fluid is forced into the soft wings, stiffening them. After a series of contractions and rest intervals, it lifts its new wings erect for the first time, and waits for them to dry. With one final contraction, the excess fluid is expelled from the body. The butterfly has become the magnificent work of art it was meant to be all along.

The purpose of the mature butterfly or moth is to bring more caterpillars into the world so the species will survive. Yet it also has a higher purpose within the web of life. It fills an ecological niche in the food chain and pollinates flowers, contributing to the well-being of all creatures on earth. For those who see it, the butterfly brings beauty to the world. It also shows us humans that transformation is a common and natural part of life's process.

＊　＊　＊

Years after my schoolteacher days, toward the end of a long and difficult marriage, I was visited in a dream by the image of a magnificent moth. Unusually large and fuzzy, it was snow-white on top with reddish fur underneath. It had a large body, feathery antennae, and delicate, sensitive nostrils. This mysterious, magical creature was much more than a moth. The image touched me deeply. In the next scene of my dream, it was in a killing jar filled with a poisonous liquid. No longer a moth, it had mutated into a small egg at the bottom of the jar. The egg slowly released tiny bubbles of air that floated to the top.

This vivid dream spoke clearly to me. The dramatic images reflected the reverse metamorphosis that had occurred in my life. Over time, the quality of my life had deteriorated. My self-esteem was in shambles. In desperation, I left my marriage and my role of housewife.

Though I was the most important person in the lives of my children, outside my role of mother I felt like a big zero. Feeling like a nobody, I didn't know that I was important, special, and capable. I never dreamt that I had within me the potential for greatness. Hidden from my consciousness, there was a wonderful plan for my life.

Cautiously, I began to rummage through the fabric of my being, examining every thread. I made a vow to be completely honest with myself. The intensity of this commitment drove me to work with two therapists and fill five journals with my writing. That was the most intense and thorough "spring cleaning" of my life. I desperately wanted to understand why—when I had done everything I was "supposed to" do—it had all gone wrong.

During this soul-searching and empowering process, I first learned about self-esteem and how to manage it in myself. Gradually

I began to thaw out frozen pieces of my being. I began to discover and design a new relationship with myself, and also with my children. Bit by bit I gained a sense of personal value, competence, and worth.

In what seemed like blind groping for new ways of being, I embarked on the intensive and extensive journey of my own transformation. Butterflies—a symbol of transformation for thousands of years—became the decorating motif of my home. They reminded me that what seemed like the end was, in reality, a new beginning. I never suspected that in some mysterious, mystical way, I was being thrust into a metamorphosis that would take me to heights I never dreamed possible.

"Every journey has a secret destination
of which the traveler is unaware."

—Martin Buber

THE CATERPILLAR'S HOME

Dysfunctional Family Systems

*"Every child has an inalienable right to
be bonded in welcoming arms, kindly initiated
into a caring culture, allowed to play freely
in the senses and imagination."*

—Sam Keen

I WENT BACK to school to get my doctorate in psychology. The common thread, I noticed, between all types of mental illness, is the lack of self-esteem. As I began to research this topic more and more, I realized that the crucial foundation for self-esteem occurs unconsciously at early ages. Either you are born into a family that values and cherishes you and meets your basic needs, or you are born into a dysfunctional family.

Dysfunctional or unhealthy family systems are the breeding ground for lifelong problems; in childhood the knots of pain are tied and are often drawn tighter as we mature. A young child's experience is generally restricted to his or her family of origin. The patterns of relationship—to self, to parents and siblings, to life itself—are learned there and considered to be "normal." If an unhealthy model is all we know, we assume that's how families are "supposed to" be. And since family patterns tend to be repeated, the problems are easily passed along from one generation to the next.

Parents in dysfunctional families tend to have certain characteristics:

- They do not fully accept themselves or others.
- They emotionally, physically, or sexually abuse their children; or they neglect them—being disinterested, unavailable, or absent.
- They don't take care of their own wants and needs or those of others.
- They are needy and expect their children to meet their needs.
- They don't know how to handle feelings and try to avoid them.
- They may be perfectionists; to them mistakes mean total failure.
- Addictions are common.
- They are inconsistent, arbitrary, unpredictable, and chaotic—or rigidly autocratic.
- They have low self-esteem.

These parents' communication patterns also tend to have the following characteristics:

- They don't listen to others. They react rather than respond.
- Their words are critical and harmful, and are loaded with judgment, discouragement, humiliation, and insults.
- They commonly make "You statements." ("You idiot!" "You always..." "You never...")
- They tend to be aggressive (bullies) or passive (doormats).
- Decisions and actions are based in fear, anger, and pain—not love.
- They neither encourage nor respect boundaries—theirs or those of others.

These problem behaviors may not be seen as problems. Or, they may be recognized as such, then denied because of the pain, the complexity, or the lack of ability to cope with them. Yet diagnosis, according to physicians, is 90 percent of the cure. Only when problems are named, can they be discussed and resolved.

In most, if not all, troubled families, some members are willing or able to see the problems, and others are not. There are many ways to respond to chronic pain. For example, one child may see that his parents are troubled, another may feel guilty or responsible. How did you respond?

*   *   *

When my husband and I were first married and madly in love, we decided that we wouldn't have problems "like other couples." With great intentions, and even greater naïveté, we assumed that marriage would mean "happily ever after" as we had been led to believe. We couldn't see that this assumption was the seed for the eventual decay of our relationship. Because we had agreed from the start to ignore our problems, we could never talk about the root causes of our discontent. It seemed to work for a long time, but our assumption of happiness could not last. We did not realize that when you deny your problems, you give up the power to overcome them.

What happens when the stork comes along and brings a present for such confused and confusing young couples? What does it feel like to be born into a family that does not know how to handle difficulties? Let's imagine Teresa, a beautiful little butterfly, who, after flying with the angels, suddenly lands in such a setting. It doesn't take long to notice that something isn't right. She soon realizes, in fact, that something is very wrong.

We all enter the world with fairly simple needs: to be protected, to be nurtured, to be loved unconditionally, and to belong. Is that asking too much? What happens to little Teresa? She gets hungry. She cries and cries, wanting someone to hold her, feed her, and fill her needs. It may or may not happen. Her parents may or may not be able to, for one reason or another that probably has nothing to do with Teresa.

When she is mistreated, she concludes that her needs are not important, that she is not lovable, that she can't trust her parents to hold up their end of the bargain. But still she has to depend on them for her very survival. Knowing something is wrong, and yet needing to believe that her parents are okay, she may come to the conclusion that *she is the problem.* Something is wrong with *her.* Her original sense of self-worth evaporates with that understanding. Everything she may do from that point on may be an attempt to cover up her sense of worthlessness or shame, and to try to convince herself that she is indeed "okay."

Did this happen to you? Putting two and two together in your pre-verbal and pre-mathematical mind, you may have figured that your parents—those all-knowing giants—were treating you as you deserved to be treated. This belief was formed before you could vote, before you could cross the street on your own, maybe before you could even feed yourself.

And then you grew up, and maintained those beliefs. That you were a burden. That you weren't allowed to talk about feelings or problems or needs. That you did not deserve unconditional love. Buried beneath all your later learnings, these beliefs got in the way of you ever reaching your butterfly potential.

Our earliest decisions, conclusions, and beliefs have the most far-reaching impact on our lives. We may never even know we have them because they are made by our pre-conscious minds and lie beyond our conscious grasp. Yet for better or worse, those primal "truths" about ourselves, our parents, and our world shape our entire lives.

Children from troubled family systems tend to develop the following characteristics:

- They can't depend on or trust their parents to fill their needs, to love them, or to protect them. Instead they are expected to fill the needs of their parents.
- Their emotional development is arrested.
- They conclude that it's not safe to be who they really are, so they pretend to be who they're not.
- They are fearful and insecure.
- They may thrive on chaos, excitement, drama, and crisis, and create these things in their lives.

- Having been victimized, they may victimize themselves and/or others.
- Lacking a sense of personal power, they look to others to tell them how they should be, or they seek power over others.
- They feel a full range of intense negative emotions such as fear, shame, abandonment, anger, resentment, distrust, disrespect, worthlessness, powerlessness, loneliness, and isolation, yet they do not know what to do with these feelings.
- They lack self-respect and have low self-esteem.

These states of being do not happen automatically, and they do not happen to everyone.

You started as a beautiful young butterfly, aware of the beauty of your own life. But if your family happened to be a dysfunctional one, you heard all sorts of strange, ugly messages about yourself. These messages were hard to believe, so you ignored them at first. You may have considered using your wings to get back to the heavens, but decided not to because you loved these people. So you concluded that you'd better adjust and adapt to the situation.

You made some decisions. You may have decided to trust your parents instead of yourself, or you may have decided that you couldn't really trust anyone (even if your life depended on it). You may have decided that you can't talk about what you feel, want, or know (because parents and/or other adults won't or don't know how to listen). And you may have concluded that your feelings were not acceptable. Not knowing what to do with them, you try to turn them off.

Children in troubled families need to protect themselves somehow, to defend and insulate themselves from their unfriendly environment. Somewhere deep down they may have a vague memory of a warm and safe cocoon, so they build up layer after layer of armor and protection. These layers create the following core issues common to many children from dysfunctional families.

- **A need to control.** Struggling to survive in a fear-full world, they learn to control and manipulate others as well as themselves. They control their feelings, behaviors, and thoughts, and their outward expression. The unpredictability and chaos of real life causes them to be on alert at all times. Hyper-vigilance results in chronic stress, producing a high level of stress hormones even when at rest. These stress hormones may become physically addictive.

- **Over-responsibility.** Children take everything personally. They believe they are treated as they deserve to be treated. Abused children figure that they've got it coming. Words such as "You make me mad" may give them an inflated and unrealistic sense of their power and responsibility for other's emotions and actions. They may even over-generalize to such a degree that they think they are responsible for all problems that happen in the family. Layer upon layer of confusion, guilt, and shame begin to build, with nothing ever being understood or forgiven.

- **Lack of trust.** When the people they love the most are not there for them, children from unhealthy families may learn that their parents—on whom their very existence depends—cannot be trusted. When they are told to stop lying, shut up, and stop crying, they learn to distrust their own perceptions, their senses, their intuition, their feelings, and their Self. They are forced to shut down these most important guides for knowing and being themselves, and for living their own lives on this planet. This cloaks them in bewilderment and confusion and builds a wall between them and the world.

- **Avoidance of feelings.** Infants and young children are totally transparent. When they are happy, their whole body collapses in laughter; when they cry, it feels like the end of the world and everyone knows it. Many parents, on the other hand, don't know what to do with their own feelings, so they don't know what to do with the feelings of their children. They may end up teaching them that feelings are wrong, bad, unimportant, and/or scary. "Big boys don't cry!" "Nice girls don't get mad!" Or they may try to manipulate a child's feelings. "Kiss and make up." "Stop crying or I'll give you something to cry about!" Children learn that feelings are to be hidden, ignored, repressed, denied, minimized, and/or eliminated. In this state of contradiction and constriction, their "wiring" may become scrambled, and intuition and healthy human functioning get lost in the shuffle.

- **Ignore personal needs.** It's the job of parents to meet the basic physical and emotional needs of their children. Emotionally troubled parents, however, fail to do this. They may even expect children to fill their needs—something that children cannot do. So kids learn that it is not safe to have needs; their needs are an imposition on others. If their needs are fulfilled, there may be strings attached. They might feel guilty in having needs, and pretend to not have them. When they get tired of being disappointed, they stop asking, stop wanting, stop needing.

- **Extremely low self-esteem.** In their world of broken promises, where their needs are minimized or ignored, children have trouble trusting, seeing things clearly, and believing in themselves. As a result, children feel worthless. If this was your story, you may have difficulty to this day realizing that you have the right

  - to be treated well

  - to set limits for yourself

  - to be happy

During my thirteen years of being a full-time, stay-at-home mom, I worked very hard to understand and turn around the dysfunctional patterns I had learned from my family of origin. I really wanted to do better with my own children, and be the parent I wish I'd had. I took my roles of wife and mother very seriously and delighted in watching my children grow in grace and strength and beauty. My husband and I had both showered our children with a lot of love. At the time of our separation, I believed that their formative years had been very healthy, and that we had prepared them well for life. Because I could no longer be with them on a daily basis, I hoped and prayed that they would be all right.

Yet change was upon us and this tumultuous change was most difficult; everything was topsy-turvy. There was a battle for custody. The arrangement was finally made that they would continue to live in their home and continue to attend their schools, while I would move to a nearby city to pursue my education and find my direction in life.

My ex-husband married a woman with three children of her own. The challenge of blending two families proved difficult for everyone involved. After a while, I began to hear stories from my children that their lives were changing dramatically. There was a great deal of tension, frustration, and lack of communication which erupted into frequent conflicts. I recognized their painful situation, yet could not be there for them as I had before.

They no longer felt like they could trust the adults in their household or talk about their problems and feelings with them. They learned to insulate themselves, and also developed survival strategies. For example, to fill their need for belonging, they joined church groups, youth clubs, teams, and the school band. They "adopted" surrogate family members to fill in the gaps. They discovered remarkable resilience and found ways to take care of themselves.

I kept in close contact with them throughout this time. As I listened to their stories and their feelings and remembered the pain from my own childhood, I tried to help them understand what was happening and offered as much support as I could. At the university, my studies turned into a quest for the ingredients of healthy families and for ways to build the self-esteem of children. I never dreamed that these traumatic events were building blocks for my transformation, and the wellspring of my passion for helping families and saving kids' lives.

Knowing that my own offspring were no longer developing in the relaxed, healthy way they had as small children, I worried that they would not be able to take the last, graceful steps required to become healthy, independent adults. Eventually, my two older children moved out to attend college, and my youngest moved in with me. For each of them, in many ways, their early adulthood has been a process of trying to catch up with themselves. My own process—reaching even into midlife—paralleled theirs. We were each struggling to grow up in our own ways.

In every area of development, whether personal, interpersonal, financial, artistic, emotional, physical, spiritual, or social, there are stages one must go through. Life is a process of passages, of casting off old knowledge and replacing it with new. In some processes, like playing the piano or learning to cook, the steps toward proficiency are more clear to us. You have to practice, practice, practice. But skills for living life itself are not always so obvious.

It is important that the foundation for human development be strong. To build anything, a house, for example, each stage must be successfully completed before proceeding to the next stage. A firm foundation must be securely in place before the framing or electrical work begins. With humans, the foundation for mental health lies in the early formative years of life. When children miss out on the essentials, their foundations shift continually beneath them, like houses built on sand. The failure to complete important developmental tasks during early childhood is the basis for codependency.

Many parents manage their lives quite successfully and are able to teach their children what they know. Yet, times can change so rapidly that their skills may lose their relevance. Others are simply lacking important life skills. Whichever kind of parents you had, you may have received limited information for figuring out how to survive your childhood, and consequently missed out on important aspects of your development.

The tasks of childhood include development of trust, autonomy, initiative, industriousness, identity, intimacy, and integrity. These are the things every child must learn in order to become a healthy adult. If you did not master these basic life skills as a child, you will not be able to solve adult problems gracefully. If you did not complete this early work, every problem—no matter how large or small—could be a major crisis for you.

You may have felt like a piece of Swiss cheese sometimes, sensing a lot of holes in your life that you did not know how to fill, too many empty spots, too many loose ends and missing pieces. In trying to fill these holes you may have made choices which seemed right at the time, but developed into addictions which further froze your development and stunted your growth.

In order to become whole, one must identify and fill in the developmental holes with the proper things. What are these things? Did you miss out on any of these?

- Bonding and unconditional love
- Nurturing and protection
- Acceptance and respect
- Protection and boundaries
- Trust in yourself and others
- Comfort with feelings
- Meeting personal needs
- Intuition and spirituality
- Encouragement, support from others, and for oneself (self-talk)
- Communication skills: listening and speaking skills
- Quality time spent with others
- Assertiveness, asking and refusal skills
- Healthy responsibility, individual and shared
- High (yet attainable) and clear expectations
- Self-awareness, self-care, and self-love

Children with high self-esteem have completed the identity-building tasks that allow them to enjoy these things in their adult lives. They are resilient. They are effective in work, in play, and in relationships. Children who are missing the self-esteem which allows such effectiveness are most at risk for alcohol and other drug-related problems.

Now, put yourself in the place of the little butterfly again. Imagine how it might have been different if:

- Your parents welcomed you and cherished you, and your relatives and neighbors danced and celebrated your blessed arrival.
- You could trust your parents to take care of your basic needs.

- You knew that your parents could and would protect you from harm.
- Your parents had your best interests in mind, and helped you to develop your judgment and intuitive skills.
- Your parents understood your need to explore, and gave you both the freedom and the limits to do so safely.
- Your parents respected and loved you just for being you, and taught you to respect yourself.
- Your parents were healthy, happy individuals who listened to you and helped you deal with your feelings.
- Your parents shared their wisdom and welcomed the wisdom you had to share as well and were respectful of your boundaries.

In such a situation, you would have learned to accept, love and respect yourself; to trust, nurture, and protect yourself. You would have learned to be aware of your needs and how to fill them. Your communication style with yourself and others would be direct, encouraging, supportive, and positive. Knowing that you were safe, you could be honest, spontaneous, and creative; you could be who you really are. You would feel like dancing—not struggling, flying—not crawling, through your life. Your self-esteem would reflect the joy that you felt being alive.

Family patterns tend to repeat until we become conscious of them, until we are uncomfortable enough to change our behavior, until we become courageous enough to break the cycle. It takes time to grow beyond the habits and crossed wiring of childhood. Many people who lacked important psychological nutrients as children become late bloomers. They fill their areas of deficiency as adults and learn new skills. Shedding the layers of caterpillar skin that they have guarded themselves with, they begin the metamorphosis into a healthy adult life. Addressing and healing the wounds of childhood allows the complete recovery of one's self-esteem. It's never too late to become the magnificent person you were meant to be.

Caterpillars do not know that they are destined to be butterflies. Yet there is a plan hidden deep within their genetic code, far beyond their consciousness, that guides them through the stages of meta-morphosis. That vague, deep memory of the butterfly you once were will also guide you through your transformation if you allow it, if you honor it, if you learn to trust it. You will rediscover your wings and let them take you to heights you only dreamed of before.

"We all start out perfect. You begin to see
that people become twisted when
their natural emotions are suppressed."
—Elizabeth Kübler Ross, *The Function of Feelings*

A World of Caterpillars

Dysfunctional Social Systems

*"Out of every crisis comes the choice to be
reborn, to reconceive ourselves as individuals,
to choose the kind of change that will help us
to grow and fulfill ourselves more completely."*

—Nena O'Neill

B Y NATURE, children are very impressionable because they have so much to learn to prepare themselves for the rest of life. Eager to learn about their world and how to be in it, they absorb everything. They look to their parents and the adults in their lives for love, protection, attention, and guidance. If they don't find these things in their family, they will seek answers from any source in order to fill their needs, satisfy their curiosity, or just to survive. Children are innocent and will believe the "truths" their experience gives them—whether they are true or not.

Youngsters need meaningful, long-term contact with caring adults to help them sort out all the conflicting and confusing messages the world gives, to develop social skills, and to learn how to trust themselves in the process. In simpler and healthier cultures, all adult members of a clan generally have the best interests of the community in mind, and share responsibility for the children. "Alternative" communities can also be healthy growing environments. In such communities parents, extended families, and other caring individuals hold a common vision and cooperatively provide support for the well-being of the children. "The nurturance of children is at risk as extended families disappear, both parents work, and more children rely on a single parent," says Marian Wright Edelman, chairman of the Children's Defense Fund. "It takes a community to raise a child."

In our nuclear-family oriented culture, however, where "normal" means one father, one mother, and 1.9 children, things are very different; children have fewer adult perspectives to influence them, and limited contact with extended family and neighbors. And with more and more children being raised by single parents, there is less family time if the parents work and too much attention from Madison Avenue and Hollywood. As a result, they have fewer real-life models from whom they can learn appropriate social skills and behaviors.

Children observe and learn from everything and everyone: parents, peers, the media, religion, teachers, and books. Trusting the world, they take it all in and believe it, especially when they're young.

Well-intentioned parents would never choose to enroll their children in the School of Hard Knocks. Yet the world is full of danger. Innocent kids are tempted, exploited, and manipulated to try tobacco, alcohol, and other drugs; they are taught to be good consumers—not good citizens—and use material goods to get what they want. They are taught social competition, perfectionism, and greed; they are surrounded with promiscuity and exposed to violence, domination, and victimization every day of their lives. They do not realize that every advertiser wants a piece of them, and that some things can tear a person, a family, or a community apart at the seams.

Children belong in families, which, ideally, serve as a sanctuary and a cushion from the world at large. Parents belong to society and are a part of that greater world. Sometimes parents are a channel to the larger society, sometimes they are a shield from it. Ideally they act as filters, guiding their children and teaching them to avoid the tempting trash. The many perspectives offered by the media need to be sorted through very carefully.

Mass-media cultural myths and values clutter minds with misinformation that can imprison people in frustration, alienation, and pain. An addictive society depends on dysfunctional families. It teaches children to relate to themselves and to others in unhealthy ways to keep the cycle going.

A healthy society, on the other hand, teaches its citizens to care for themselves and others, to be responsible, and to have concern for the common good. A healthy community cares for, protects, and looks out for its young. Children need a number of caring adults to guide and temper them, to show them decency, compassion, and love. The essential life skills children learn from their models will help them to become secure, healthy, and caring grown-ups themselves.

When I finally made the decision to leave my painful caterpillar life behind, one of the greatest obstacles I had to overcome was my own self-judgment. I was raised to believe that the only appropriate path for a woman's life was the one I was on—that of wife and mother. My parents both had a grade-school education in Germany and did not value higher education, especially for girls. They did not believe I needed an education to find a husband and have babies. I had to overcome their resistance to go to college.

I had only one relative who had been educated. She was a teacher and a principal. As a role model, she inspired me and helped convince my parents to give me the permission I sought. My brief career as an elementary school teacher was regarded as temporary until my "real" career in motherhood got started. My parents were greatly relieved when my first child came along. So when I divorced my husband after a sixteen-year marriage and the kids lived with him while I attended graduate school, the weight of all their beliefs were against me. It was not "okay" for me to want to be more than a homemaker.

In subtle and blatant ways we learn the values and judgments of our families, schools, and our society in general; as children, we learn who and what is okay and who and what is not. The "okay" list is all too often rather short: to be beautiful or handsome, and popular; to be wealthy and white. You've heard the saying: "You can't be too rich or too thin." According to these standards, few people, if any, are really okay! Even the most successful, beautiful models who are held up to us as standards of perfection have low self-esteem; they know about their moles, warts, and other flaws that have been air-brushed out of the picture. They have inner doubts and demons just like the rest of us.

The "not-okay" list, on the other hand, can be extensive. As children, we may have learned to look down on (and put down) certain people:

- foreigners • people of color • those who speak differently • members of other churches • "sinners" • the poor • the rich • people who are too tall or too short • women and girls who are not "beautiful" • girls who are smarter than boys • people who stray out of rigid gender-role definitions • people who dress in last year's styles • people with alcoholism, incest, abuse, or suicide in their families • homeless people • people who eat with the wrong fork • divorced women and men • people on welfare • Vietnam veterans • disabled, deformed, or handicapped people • homosexuals • people with cancer, AIDS, and other chronic physical or mental illnesses • fat people • old people • children and teenagers • shy people • bullies • people who drive the "wrong" car • people with bad teeth, bad breath, or body odor •

You can probably add to this list. It goes on and on and changes with every generation, every culture, subculture, and family.

In addition to the list of not-okay characteristics, we are becoming aware of the commonplace exploitation and abuse of children, women, and the earth. We are aware of the horrors of war and the decimation of native peoples, which haunt victim and "victor" alike. We see the unjust systems that exploit and enslave people and add layer upon layer to the shadow of shame that burdens our hearts. The collection of familial, cultural, and religious shame is passed down from generation to generation. It's often hard to find a proud foot to stand on.

Growing up, we internalized the numerous "original sins" that proved we were not worthwhile, not okay. We may have learned to feel shameful about our bodies and souls, about ourselves and our families, about our race or ethnic group. My parents had left Germany, not wanting to be part of Hitler's Reich. Even so, during the war my family was accused of being Nazi. As a child, I had night-mares filled with the related confusion, guilt, shame, and fear I didn't understand.

We may also learn to feel shameful *from* our families, our churches, our schools, and our peer groups. No one is spared from feelings of shame. Everyone has skeletons in their personal, family, or cultural closet, or feels as though they themselves are "in the closet" about something secret or shameful. Yet, it's very difficult to accept and love ourselves and have high self-esteem if we believe that we are defective.

In order to have mental health, healthy families, and healthy societies, every man, woman, and child needs to have positive self-esteem—a real sense of personal worth. Yet, we have built a long, established tradition into society of convincing ourselves that we are not okay. The most devastating aspect of the problem is that mostly the shame is connected with *who we are*—which we cannot change. We cannot change our nationality, color, or height, for example. Feeling defective, we might have disowned certain "not okay" parts of ourselves, such as our family, intelligence, spirituality, sexual orientation, body, or disability. Splitting off pieces of ourselves—dismembering facets of our character, history, or personality—traps us in helplessness, confusion, and despair. As we disown parts of ourselves, we lose our integrity and our sense of wholeness.

Not wanting to feel the weight of the primal burden of not-okay-ness, we try to hide our shame from others, even from ourselves. We may become dishonest and pretend to be who we are not. Or, we may try to shoulder the load and apologize our way through life. Perhaps we overcompensate and wear ourselves out trying to erase the shame. We may think that if only we were "perfect," then we would be okay. If we could only make the world perfect, then it would be okay. We may become controlling and try to force things to be as we think they should be. We may create unattainable expectations and then fail, which proves what we knew all along—we really *are* defective.

No matter what we tried to do, it seemed as if more and more layers were added to weigh down our heart and soul and damage our self-esteem. We lost trust in our family. We lost trust in society. We lost our faith. A man I know lamented, "I was so worthless, God didn't even like me. He abandoned me. I decided there couldn't be a God; how could he have allowed this to happen to me?" We lost trust in ourselves—in our judgments, feelings, and intuition—and created more holes in our being. We created a sham to erase our shame. The struggle to keep some remnants of self-worth or esteem became constant.

While caterpillars are munching away, enjoying growth spurts and casting off the old skin, we were adding layers of pain and defenses to our lives. The weight of this "protection" may have frozen our development into a cocoon-like state of limbo.

Every person wants and needs to feel important, capable, lovable, and worthwhile. In order to recover self-esteem, we must be willing to move from shame and self-rejection to acceptance and self-love. We are not profane beings, but sacred. If we have sinned, it is because we have forgotten we are blessed. We have bought a bill of goods that has made us very sick. We have missed the mark. We have been convinced that we are supposed to be caterpillars forever, and never transform into butterflies.

Yet now we have the opportunity to look at ourselves with new eyes, to reclaim and "re-member" the missing pieces of who we are. We *are* lovable. We *are* valuable. We *are* precious. We *are* and *have always been* okay just the way we are; we have done our best given the information we had at the time.

Where we have done wrong, we can learn to do right. Where we have made mistakes, we can clean them up. Where we have caused harm, we can acknowledge it and learn to heal. And where we are innocent, we should treasure it, not hide it.

Imagine how the world would be different for you if:

- Your mother and father had given you freedom to stretch the wings of your spirit while protecting you, and pointed out dangers and pitfalls without frightening you.
- You had aunts and uncles, brothers and sisters, neighbors, teachers, and friends who cared about you and helped you learn the life skills you needed to know.

- The important adults in your life had given you their undivided attention and support in the things you wanted to do, and given you the guidance you needed through the tough times.

- These adults had taught you right from wrong and had provided examples of healthy, happy lives.

- You were allowed and encouraged to learn skills for dealing with relationships, jobs, money, and other things, and to discover techniques that were all your own.

- You were allowed to make your own mistakes and learn from them.

- As you got older, you had caring mentors who helped you find your place in the world doing what you wanted to do.

- Your family was wise enough to know when they should help and when you had to learn to help yourself.

Many people did have these things, but many more, unfortunately, did not. Those who did may have been butterflies all along. They may be the ones who most inspired us (or made us most jealous!) with their freedoms, and their effortless, beautiful, creative lives. Those who did not have such support may have become caterpillars first.

LOOKING FOR SELF-ESTEEM IN ALL THE WRONG PLACES

Basic Needs and Getting Them Met

"If I were to search for the central core
of difficulty in people ... it is that
in the great majority of cases they
despise themselves, regard themselves
as worthless and unlovable....
In some instances that is covered by
pretension, and in nearly all of us
these feelings are covered by some
kind of a facade."

—Carl Rogers

MUNCHING ALONG wearily through their lowly life, caterpillars might notice butterflies soaring freely overhead. One or two of the envious ones might try to be like them. They paste on wings and jump from the trees! But instead of flying, they fall. People with low self-esteem tend to do the same, and paste on layer upon layer of embellishment, trying to be what they are not. They hope to gain approval from others so that they can feel good about themselves. For caterpillars and humans alike, this can be self-defeating.

Simply defined, self-esteem means esteeming yourself. Yet many people have the mistaken belief that their self-worth comes from people or things outside themselves. They believe that others are responsible for their happiness, then blame others for their unhappiness. For adults, however, self-esteem is determined not by what others think of you but by what you think about yourself.

People look for self-esteem in all the wrong places, through:

- **What they do.** Doing too much for others (often at their own expense), many persons are more "human doings" than human beings.

- **What they have.** Confusing "net worth" with "self worth," many collect money and possessions and can never get enough. Their favorite bumper sticker reads, "Whoever Dies With the Most Toys Wins."

- **What they know.** Trying to impress others with facts and figures, some define their identity by the degrees they've earned, the places they've been, the books they've read, and they let you know. They believe that these things make them better than others.

- **Who they know.** Name-droppers and celebrity-seekers may feel their "borrowed" status gives them more importance.

- **How they perform.** Some people put on an act in order to gain friends and influence people.

- **How they look.** Investing a great deal of time, effort, and money in their appearance, some individuals equate self-esteem with how attractive they are to others.

- **Who they are with.** Other persons think that only with a beautiful or desirable partner, or the "right" group (church, political party, school, club) will they be okay.

Any of these—doing a good job, looking good, being funny, having beautiful friends—can be an important *part* of our self-esteem, especially if these things are a genuine complement to our well-being.

The problem arises, however, if we feel we *have* to impress or please others to prove that we are okay.

If we *depend on approval* from others in order to feel we are worth something, we give up power over our own *self*-esteem. Demanding or manipulating for approval is also an attempt to control others; we may fish for compliments, but if we "catch" one we probably won't believe it. The path to self-esteem comes from gaining our *own* approval and affirming our own worth.

Self-esteem and love go hand-in-hand. But if I believe that I am not lovable, it's hard to imagine that anyone else might really love me—even when they really do and make every effort to show me. If I despise myself, I can't love my kids, my spouse, my siblings, my parents, or my friends. And if I don't care *for* myself, I don't take very good care *of* myself.

On the other hand, when I do love myself I become more loving and lovable. When I cherish myself, I take good care of myself and have an increased sense of personal worth. All my relationships, in turn, are enhanced. Unconditional self-esteem is based on unconditional love for oneself.

Remember, *self-esteem is an inside job*. As Eleanor Roosevelt said, "No one can make you feel inferior without your consent!" You alone are responsible for your own self-esteem.

- Only *you* can give yourself *self*-respect.
- Only *you* can give yourself *self*-acceptance.
- Only *you* can give yourself *self*-esteem.

And *you alone are responsible for your self-esteem*.

Self-esteem means esteeming yourself. It means knowing and affirming that you are valuable, lovable, worthwhile, and capable. It involves respecting yourself—and teaching others to respect you. It means treating others respectfully because they deserve it.

Years ago, before self-esteem was a popular concept, the world seemed to be divided into "egotists" and people with "inferiority complexes." While egotists would put others down, those with inferiority complexes would put themselves down. Naturally, the two generally came in pairs. And both suffered from low self-esteem. The egotists would put others down in order to feel better than, bigger than, and smarter than everyone else. They would think "I'm a winner; you're not so hot." "I am right so your point of view is completely worthless." The ones with inferiority complexes would accept their one-down position, because that was the only way they knew to be accepted. *When you have self-esteem, when you are okay with yourself, you don't need to make others wrong or put them down.*

Low self-esteem doesn't feel good. In fact, it aches. And what does our high-speed society teach us to do with pain and discomfort?

- Deny. Like the time I fell skiing, felt pain, and thought, "it's nothing." I stood on my broken leg, compounding the fracture, and passed out.

- Distract. When our favorite show comes on TV, we may immerse ourselves with the story of the day and forget our problems and concerns.

- Drug ourselves or take a drink to put ourselves out of our misery.

Everyone uses these strategies of avoidance at times. They can provide a brief vacation and give us time to regroup. But they can also get us into big trouble. Wanting to forget or control pain, people drink, take drugs, smoke, or eat. Wanting to feel "high," people do drugs. But the positive feelings are short lived. Drugs can stop the pain of low self-esteem, but can do nothing to raise it. These strategies of avoidance are actually the highway to chronic pain and addictions, a vicious, self-defeating cycle. When we deny, distract, or drug ourselves, we do nothing about our true problems and nothing really changes.

We need, instead, to let go and accept the fact that pain and discomfort are a part of life. They are messengers bearing important information. Instead of denying, distracting, or drugging ourselves, we need to pay attention to the tension and/or pain. What is the problem? What is the message? What is not right? What do I need to change in my life? When we identify our problems and do something, we take responsibility for ourselves. We change something, learn something, gain personal power and—voilá!—our self-esteem goes up a few notches.

Self-esteem creates natural highs. Knowing that you're lovable helps you to love more. Knowing that you're important helps you to make a difference to others. Knowing that you are capable empowers you to create more. Knowing that you're valuable and that you have a special place in the universe is a serene spiritual joy in itself.

Imagine what your life would be like if you knew that:

- You are more lovable and beautiful than you know.

- You are more powerful and important than you think.

- You are the source of your own *self*-esteem.

- You can choose the path through life that you desire.

- You are responsible for yourself first and foremost.

- *YOU REALLY ARE OKAY JUST THE WAY YOU ARE!*

Positive self-esteem is the choice to respect, accept, and love yourself fully. It is a commitment to yourself, and the best gift that you can give and receive.

PART II

THE COCOON

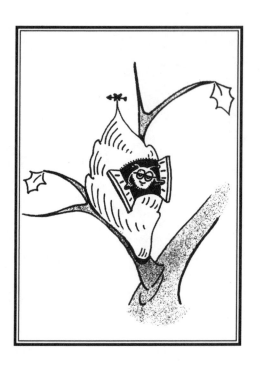

RECOVERING SELF-ESTEEM SKILLS

"There's no place like...a cocoon,
for incubating, meditating,
waiting for the right moment
to emerge... and fly away."

—Louise Hart

ONE FINE SPRING day a caterpillar decided to go for a walk. Ready to begin, it wondered which foot to move first. It thought and thought, and finally got so confused about the way things worked that it never took a single step! Soon the fine spring day was gone. Come fall, this same caterpillar decided to start spinning a cocoon. It crawled around and around, examining the tree from top to bottom in search of the perfect branch to which it could attach itself. It searched and searched but was never satisfied. Soon the fall day was gone and the weather turned cold.

Recovering self-esteem can feel like that. Our lives and inner selves are so complex that it is very difficult to unravel the root causes of self-doubt or low self-esteem. The task at hand is achieving self-awareness, which is often confused with self-consciousness. Like the caterpillars, we can get in our own way. The frustration and confusion that precede self-knowledge can trigger addictions, and addictions can keep us from self-knowledge.

At a recent book signing, a stranger poured out her story to me. Joy used to be crippled and overweight, and walked with a cane. She was constantly depressed, had daily headaches, and was even diagnosed as "manic." She overused alcohol and was addicted to Valium and cigarettes. A suicide attempt at the age of twenty-five was a turning point for her; she realized that she did not want to die. And then she took the first step.

Joy quit Valium, eliminated sugar from her meals, and changed to a macrobiotic diet. She read lots of books and started doing yoga from a tape. She set goals and re-channelled all the energy that had been dissipated by the kind of food she'd been eating. Feeling better, she then added bodywork twice weekly, got acupuncture treatments, and began to walk up to eight miles a day. In her visualization, she imagined herself striding along without the cane.

Not knowing where this journey was taking her, she certainly was enjoying the adventure. Remembering her mother's words that she was about as graceful as a horse, she even took ballet lessons at age forty-nine.

After "getting rid of a bunch of extra baggage," as she puts it, Joy is forty pounds lighter and teaches yoga classes twice a week. "These experiences led me to a peaceful journey—and I want to teach others, especially children, that there are ways to get high and find peace without drugs." Now, with no more headaches, cane, or depression, she reflected, "it's been a wonderful transformation." Her life is now, as she describes it, "a tad above excellent!"

Part II of this book is about the process of building a "cocoon" and growing within it. It contains topics, skills, and exercises that can serve as stepping stones to guide you on the pathway to discovering and recovering your self-esteem—to becoming a butterfly. There are enough activities that you can focus on one each day for a month, or select those that are most helpful to you at any given time.

Sometimes in life we need to stop the busyness to quiet our minds and sort things out. Sometimes we need to go back a few steps in order to move forward. Sometimes we need to shed what we don't want in order to make room for what we *do* want.

Futurist Faith Popcorn predicted the trend of "cocooning" in the 90s. Cocooning means "the impulse to go inside when it just gets too tough and scary outside," or, "to pull a shell of safety around yourself so you're not at the mercy of a mean, unpredictable world...." She may be referring to the urge to stay home and watch the VCR instead of going out to a movie, but the process of going inside can be a spiritual one, too. A cocoon provides a sanctuary for the complex process of metamorphosis to take hold. As humans we must find or design our own safe space for doing this important inner work. Metamorphosis may seem to be dramatic, happening all at once. In reality, it is a series of many little changes that are often hidden to the eye.

We are called to shift gears. We need to put aside our fixation on the externals and go within. During the process of inner exploration, we can look for the missing pieces of our lives and learn how to fill them in. We may even discover remnants of our forgotten wings. It takes courage to respond to the call of life, of growth, of transformation. But from the moment you take the first step toward recovery and begin to direct your own life, your days as a caterpillar are numbered.

"Whatever you can do, or dream you can do, do it.
Boldness has genius, magic, and power in it.
Begin it now."

—Goëthe

6

REACHING IN

*"It takes courage to grow up and
turn out who you really are."*

—e.e. cummings

WHAT LIES AT the very center of your universe? What is most important? What influences your actions more than anything else? Your family? Your job? Your television? Your car? Probably not, because all these things are extensions of yourself. What lies at the center is *you.*

There is an exercise called the "circle of caring." Draw a few concentric circles on a page. In the one at the very center, put your name. Inside the next closest circle, put the names of your loved ones—the ones you would miss most if anything happened to them—and also the work that is dearest to your heart. In the next circle, put the names of your friends, and in the next circle, your acquaintances. The further out you go, the more replaceable the relationships are. Where might you put your possessions? Everything in the circles is important to you, but you care about some things more than others. This exercise illustrates your priorities. They are different for everyone. But there is one that is non-negotiable: You, the subject, are at the center.

You are the source, the point-of-view, and the boss of your own life. Every decision you make affects you. So if you want to make changes in your life, where do you start? You start with you.

Listen to Yourself

"Let me listen to me and not to them."

—Gertrude Stein

We give ourselves messages about ourselves all the time, even though we may not realize it. Much of that talk originates in childhood, with the voices of people important to us. "Girls aren't smart." "You're never going to be good enough." "Fatty, fatty, two-by-four!" Sometimes these messages come in words, sometimes in feelings. Over time, this self-talk can become self-fulfilling.

Self-talk is that most important and powerful inner voice that we hear in our thoughts or just beneath them. It has tremendous impact on our emotions, actions, and the results we produce in life. The tone of our inner dialogue determines if we are our own best friend or our own worst critic.

Our beliefs, our self-image, our self-concept, and our self-esteem are all controlled by what we repetitiously tell ourselves. We think our "truths" are givens, yet:

- We can think things that are not true.
- We can think things that cause us stress.
- We can think things that make us suffer.

The truth is, we can think whatever we want.

We either encourage or discourage ourselves. We lift ourselves up or put ourselves down. We relive our history or we change its course. With our self-talk, we plant seeds in our unconscious that will grow in our lives.

People who keep telling themselves how awful, incapable, or unlucky they are really believe it. Without realizing it, they are destroying their self-esteem. Those who were blamed and criticized a lot as children probably internalized those negative statements and replay the "stinkin' thinkin'" as if it were an endlessly looping cassette tape. The problem with self-talk is that the volume is so low that mostly we don't hear it. Only when we consciously "tune in" and turn up the volume can we listen objectively to those old messages and begin to free ourselves of their grip on our life. When we change how we think about ourselves, the world around us also changes. When we change our minds, we change our life.

Exercises:

- When you're looking in the bathroom mirror today, turn up the volume on your thoughts. What are they telling you?
- Do this as much as possible today. Listen for every "I can't...," "I'm not good enough...," "If only I didn't...," "I wish I had...," and write them down.
- Watch for the very big words—such as "never" and "always".

If you have trouble tuning in, find a quiet place to sit or walk for awhile so you can listen to your self-talk.

Turn Negatives Into Positives

"When life gives you lemons, make lemonade!"

—Anonymous

Psychologist Aaron Beck characterized the self-talk of his patients in terms of themselves, the world, and the future. Depressed patients' points of view were generally internal ("it was my fault"), global ("it affects everything"), and stable ("it always happens this way"). Healthier people, by contrast, saw things externally ("it was the circumstance"), specific ("it's only one thing"), and transitory ("it'll be different tomorrow").

Once you know what you're saying to yourself, you can begin to change the messages. *With awareness comes choice.* Sometimes it's enough just to notice your thoughts and acknowledge them: "Oh, I hear a voice that tells me I'm too dumb to speak up." When you write down the hurtful messages, you can view them differently and get perspective on them. Put those negative thoughts to work *for* you by turning them into positive affirmations. Here are a few examples:

Negative messages	Changed into affirmations
"Don't talk."	*"I have important things to say."*
"I look so fat!"	*"I love my body and feel good."*
"You can't do anything right."	*"I succeed when I put my mind to it."*
"Don't expect too much."	*"I'll make my dreams come true."*
"I'm not good enough."	*"I am good!"*

Sometimes people who are aware of their "voices" will try to argue their way out of the criticism. When you struggle with a voice that tells you you're no good, however, you give it power. You can't talk back to these voices. They always win. If you ignore them, they will find another way to be heard. On the other hand, if you *replace* them with affirmations, you will find yourself winning in all areas of your life.

Exercises:

- Talk back to your self-talk! See what it feels like to slip in an affirmation whenever you hear a negative message. It may feel like a lie at first. Experiment with it anyway, and challenge yourself to see the truth in it. You might see some surprising results.

- Stop the stinkin' thinkin'. You might say "Cancel, cancel!" to erase negative statements whenever they occur.

- Instead of berating yourself for what you *should have done*, think instead about what you *could have done*. Plan how you would say or do it differently (and better) if you got the chance.

- Use positive self-talk to talk about and create *what you do want in your life*. Encourage and support your progress. Affirmations can help you to move from "I can't" to "Of course I can!"

This may not seem easy to do, but it really is. You can put an end to your negative thinking by letting it go and replacing it with positive thinking. You don't have to put up with put-downs—especially from yourself.

Give Yourself a Break: Acknowledge Your Qualities

"If I am not for myself, who will be?"

—Hillel

For years, Mr. Rogers has been telling children, "You are special!" This message is true for kids, and it's also true for adults. You are okay—and always have been. But can you think of five examples of what makes you special? How about ten? Many adults are hard-pressed to come up with even one.

Exercises:

- Write on a piece of paper, "I'm terrific because..." Complete the sentence as many times as you can. Does "trustworthy" fit? How about "caring"? Do you like yourself for being funny? Athletic? Friendly? When you get five sentences completed, go for ten. You may notice your negative self-talk protesting loudly as you do this. Do it anyhow. And remember there are no wrong answers!

- Or you can do this exercise with someone else. Face your partner, look him or her in the eyes and ask, "How are you terrific?" They respond by saying, "I'm terrific because..." and finishing the sentence as many times as possible for three or four minutes. The listener might write down some of those special qualities. Then switch so both of you can play. I use this game in every one of my workshops. (Everyone *loves* listening to the terrific messages. Saying them, however, makes many people uncomfortable. It does get easier with practice.)

- On separate pieces of paper, write down every important compliment that you have received over the years. Gather up all the love notes and thank you notes that people have given you. Put them in a special "Compliment Box." (You can recycle any box for this, or use a bag or even a folder). Keep this box near your bed. When you are feeling "down," read as many as necessary until you are feeling "up."

Accept Yourself Just the Way You Are

"The curious paradox is that when I accept myself
just as I am, then I can change."

—Carl Rogers

Humans, like caterpillars, come in different sizes, shapes, and colors. Unlike caterpillars, we can spend time and energy rejecting, hating, denying parts (or all) of who we are—and create dissatisfaction, pain, and even mental illness in the process. Jesus recommended we be like "the lilies of the field." Let's learn self-acceptance from the flowers and birds and caterpillars.

The word *accept* is from a Latin root meaning to receive or "take to oneself." This is the most basic need you had as a child—to be embraced or welcomed just the way you were. Acceptance is the basis for safety, for trust, for love, for self-esteem. If you received it from your parents, you received a great gift. If not, you can heal that old wound by giving it to yourself. Open your heart and be more gentle, understanding, and compassionate with yourself. It's okay to be just you. In fact, it's imperative. If you aren't who you are, who will be?

In our consumer society, we've been taught that no one is really okay. We need one more product, one more thing before we can be happy like the fantasy folks on TV. We've been taught to reject and dislike ourselves the way we are now. This is a cause for the epidemic of low self-esteem. Yet acceptance is different from liking. Accepting yourself does not mean approving of shoddy behaviors (like abusing others or addiction). When you honestly confront and deal with those problem areas and overcome them, you become more acceptable to yourself.

With acceptance, we make the stand to be *for*, not *against*, ourselves. With acceptance, we come home to ourselves, breathe more easily, and then, *if we choose to*, we can make some changes. In totally accepting ourselves, we begin to discover that the child within is not such a bad kid after all.

Exercises:

- List some things you don't like about yourself. For example, "I don't like the mole on my nose." "I don't like that I don't fit in." "I don't like that I eat when I'm bored." "I don't like that I am afraid to travel."

- Read each sentence adding, "...and I accept myself just the way I am." Repeat this exercise a few times. Do this whenever you hear those critical voices.

- If there is something about you that you can accept but would still like to change, like getting the mole removed, getting your teeth fixed, or losing weight, do it!

- Inside yourself is a memory of the child who was not accepted and was hurt. Use your imagination to receive and embrace that child, and reassure it with your adult knowledge, understanding, and compassion. Give it what it needs.

Accept Feelings

"Conflict, pain, tension, fear, paradox..., these are transformations trying to happen. Once we confront them, the transformative process begins."

—Marilyn Ferguson, *The Aquarian Conspiracy*

At some time or other, everyone has experiences that create feelings too powerful to bear. These emotions can become blocked and remain hidden until we are in a more powerful place and are ready to face them. Part of recovery is allowing a safe time and place to feel and heal hidden feelings. In our culture, it is frequently not safe to express feelings; doing so can put us in danger. So, in order to survive and thrive, we need to know when to reveal them and when to keep them in check.

Feelings are valid. Listen to them. They are our guides through the human experience. Honor them. Like an ever-changing barometer, emotions reflect the quality of our life experiences.

When feelings are frozen, they may become distorted. As they thaw out, a support group or therapist can help us to get through the backlog and learn healthy ways of dealing with them. Like healthy children, every adult is potentially able to participate fully in the range of emotion that the human experience is all about.

Befriend your feelings. They mean that you are alive! Allow the pain, the anger, the joy, the sadness. Acknowledge them. Tell someone about them or write about them. Decide if, when, and how you want to act on them.

Be in charge of your feelings—so they won't be in charge of you. You can only do this if you know and understand them. This does not happen overnight; it takes time to become emotionally mature. We need to be able to feel, to be real, to be honest, to be who we really are with ourselves and the most important people in our lives.

Exercises:

- Humans experience many different feelings in a day. In your journal, take notes of some of the emotions you felt in the last day or two. When did you feel them? Where in your body did you experience them? Describe what you noticed. What did you do with them? Did they remind you of anything? Are any feelings missing from your day?

- Do you have any feelings toward others that are unresolved, that you don't understand or can't accept? Write about them.

Self-Care

"Where you tend a rose, a thistle cannot grow."

—Frances Hodgson Burnett

Each person is issued only one body in this lifetime. Our bodies and selves are complex systems of energy and matter that require maintenance. Without food, we starve. Without water, we dehydrate. Our bodies need proper nutrition and care or they work against us. So do the other aspects of our beings. Mental, emotional, spiritual, and physical health go hand in hand.

I was taught that self-neglect and self-sacrifice are virtues. Raised traditionally, I learned to take care of everyone else's needs at the expense of my own. Many people—especially women—have learned to give and give until it hurts, then to give some more. They are in danger of becoming long-suffering martyrs. They are at risk of emotional and physical bankruptcy and burnout. Other people—especially men—get in the habit of proving and proving, until it hurts, and then proving themselves some more.

Instead of such self-neglect and self-abuse, be good to yourself. Indulge yourself. Human beings need to be handled with care. It is your responsibility to take very good care of yourself. It's your job to make your life enjoyable.

Exercises:

- Get a pencil and paper and set aside ten uninterrupted minutes. Across the top of the page, write, "Twenty Things I Love to Do." Down the left side, number 1 to 20.

- Now for the fun part: Think about and list the things you love to do. Some will be things to do alone, some with others.

- Look at this list, and note when you last did each thing.

- Next, cross off any that are bad for you, or unhealthy (too dangerous, expensive, wasteful, hurtful to others, and so on.). If your list is now empty, start over and be more creative.

- And then do the really fun part. Every day do at least one of those things for yourself. When you are good *to* yourself, you feel good *about* yourself. Self-care boosts your energy and awareness, raises your self-esteem, and feeds your soul.

Attend to Your Needs

"The enlightened man eats when he is hungry
and sleeps when he's tired."

—Zen saying

In order to have high self-esteem, you must take good care of yourself. This entails knowing what your needs are, identifying the signals, and knowing how to meet them. According to psychologist Abraham Maslow, needs are arranged in a hierarchy. The basic human needs, in order of appearance, are:

- food, water, and clothing
- safety and shelter
- cherishing and belonging
- self-esteem
- self-actualization

According to Maslow, you cannot reach self-actualization if your most basic needs of food and shelter are unfulfilled. Like climbing a ladder, in order to get to the top, we need to climb the rungs below.

Many people from dysfunctional families often don't realize when they're hungry, tired, sleepy, or when they have to go to the bathroom. Perhaps they are so busy taking care of others, they neglect themselves. Perhaps they deny their needs in order to avoid being vulnerable; they may have gotten tired of too many disappointments and stopped asking or stopped needing. Perhaps they heard, "You don't know what you want!" and believed it.

The media has blurred the distinction even further. We have all been manipulated into "needing" things that we had gotten along very nicely without. It's important to sort through this confusion and become aware of our body, emotions, and spirit, and learn how to care for our basic needs.

Exercises:

- Start by sitting quietly for a few minutes. Scan your body from head to toe. How's your neck? Your back? Your stomach? Where are you comfortable? Stressed? Tight? Relaxed?

- Is there a connection between your thoughts and their relationship to your body's sensations? For example, when you go back for that tenth cookie, who or what is on your mind? Do your hands get cold or hot when you balance your checkbook?

- Try something new to heighten your body awareness. A fast, a cold shower, or a run can quickly bring things into focus. Yoga or martial arts—which integrate the mind and body—may be worth pursuing at some time in your life.

Feed Your Body, Feed Your Spirit

"No disease is all in your mind."

—Michael Lesser, M.D.

Good nutrition is crucial for self-care. It is essential for health—physical, emotional, and mental. Because the brain and body function by means of chemical reactions, most addictions are aggravated by nutritional imbalances, and control of them is easier with the help of a good diet. Just as being hungry can make you cranky and negative, healthy food can help you maintain a positive attitude toward life.

Traditionally, a mother passed on cooking skills to her daughters, effectively training them for their "job" in life—to feed their husbands and children. Roles today are no longer so strict. Yet there comes a time in each of our lives when we must learn to care for and feed ourselves, because if we don't, no one is going to do it for us. Yet very few young men or women are taught, consciously, how to prepare and eat food that will maintain maximum health.

Americans spend billions every year trying to lose weight. Whether they actually are overweight or simply perceive themselves as fat, they preoccupy themselves with weight-loss techniques that may or may not be effective. But a diet is not a temporary thing you go on; your diet is what you eat every day. Whether it sustains or degrades health is the question. The fast pace of American life—combined with its fixation on images—creates tensions and expectations around food that make it an issue for self-esteem.

Exercises:

- Read the labels on food packages. Do you know what all the ingredients are? Can you even pronounce them? What effect will they have on your body?

- Keep a food diary for a week. How do you feel after you eat a plum? A hamburger? Chocolate? Our bodies are constantly giving us feedback. When we eat foods that are not good for us, they tell us. Notice how food makes you feel.

- Think about *how* you've eaten in the last few days. Did you taste your food? Did you enjoy it? Did you eat because you were hungry or for another reason?

- How much time do you spend eating? Do you while standing up, while driving your car, while watching TV? Do you jump up and down at the dinner table serving others? Or do you sit down and relax, and savor your meals? Before your next meal, pause to reflect on the work that went into producing and preparing the food. Notice the aroma. Take in the color. Think about where it came from. Savor the different flavors. Chew every bite until it's liquified. Be grateful that you have food to eat.

- Learn about your body. Find out if you have food addictions or allergies. Seek out information that will help you more easily live with yourself.

- Eat a low-fat, high-fiber balanced diet of delicious, healthy food. It can lighten your spirits and help you soar!

Stay in Motion

"Sound mind, sound body."

—Proverb

The ancients viewed the body as a vehicle to carry the spirit through life on this earth. You can trust your body to keep you alive in the most basic ways: you don't have to think to breathe, to make your heart beat, or to digest your food. And your body has to trust you to feed it properly, keep it clean and out of danger, and keep it fit.

Exercise improves physical, emotional, and mental health by keeping the metabolic system in tune, giving you time for yourself, and making you breathe hard. Regular physical exercise can improve your mental outlook, help you deal with stress better, keep your organs healthy, and in effect, help you live better and longer. Besides, it can be fun.

In earlier rural societies, out-of-doors physical activity was the way of life. After you kneaded bread, hand-washed the laundry and hung it out to dry, and planted a garden, there was no need to go to aerobics. Now, the conveniences of modern life have brought us indoors and made us sedentary. So for physical well-being, activities must be consciously structured into our days.

Exercises:

- Exercise! The hardest part is overcoming inertia and getting started.
- There are hundreds of ways to build fitness into your daily regime. You can join an exercise program or get aerobics videotapes. Try taking morning walks or evening runs. Consider taking up dancing, martial arts, weight training, swimming, fencing, or any number of other activities, which you can do alone or in a group. Follow your interests.
- Opinions differ on the amount of exercise we need. One source says fifteen minutes a day is all it takes to make the difference between being fit and being fat. Another recommends 30 minutes three times a week as the minimum. Still another says 45 minutes four times a week can help you lose weight fastest. A friend of mine simply tries to get her heart beating fast at least once a day. Find out what works for you. Then do it!

Quit

"You can't solve a problem at the same level that it was created. You have to rise above it to the next level."

—Albert Einstein

How do you know you have a problem? Many people use alcohol sparingly, to relax or to celebrate, without being addicted to it. But there is a difference between eating a piece of cake and having to eat it.

There is a difference between using substances and abusing substances. There is a difference between wanting something and needing it.

Some people have greater tendencies toward addiction than others. Addictions can be physical or emotional. Addiction is about trying to fill holes. Recovery is about shrinking holes. Quitting means giving up the substance. Recovery is about giving up addictive behaviors.

There is no easy way to give up an addiction. Each substance has its own personality. For example, you can find a way to avoid drugs or alcohol altogether in your life, but you cannot entirely give up food. Sex is another natural urge that needs dealing with. But behaviors in both of these areas can be consciously changed through the work of recovery. The key to mastering any addiction is learning to live in a world *with* alcohol, drugs, sex, and food, not *for* them.

The concept of "recovery" was originally used in the context of addictive substances such as drugs or alcohol. Recovery begins after you quit. When you get tired of the life your addiction creates for you and decide to leave it behind, the first step is quitting. "Not drinking is the single most important thing I've done in my life," said a friend, "and what I have to do every day." After the initial step of quitting, the real work of recovery is the day-by-day path toward self-knowledge.

Dave had a reputation for wild parties and high times. He broke his knee while doing drugs, but that did not make him quit. He lost a best friend in a drunk-driving accident, but that did not make him quit. When he realized that he was losing *all* his best friends because of his drunken late-night phone calls and temper tantrums, things began to change.

Dave finally became aware of the fact that his lifestyle depended on substance abuse, and he decided to go sober. When my daughter heard the news, she was excited. "Good!" she said, "He can have my phone number again!" Last fall, after celebrating nearly six years of sobriety, we celebrated their marriage. The rewards of recovery are great!

Exercises:

- Watch your habits for a while. Do you become a "different person" after drinking or using drugs, one that you would not choose to be if you were sober? If you're ready for the truth, ask a friend to tell you, honestly, what you're like under the influence.

- Check out your body chemistry. A chemical imbalance can promote cravings for alcohol, drugs, tobacco, and sugar, which in turn deplete your body of essential vitamins and minerals, and create a catch-22 of disease. A physician or health practitioner can help you to get more information on nutrition.

- Alcoholics Anonymous has helped millions of people in the recovery process. Other support groups that use similar methods for recovery are Narcotics Anonymous, Overeaters Anonymous, Alanon (for spouses of alcoholics), Alateen, and Adult Children of Alcoholics. Call the AA number in the phone book for more information on open meetings near you.

Examine Your "Truths"

"Whether you believe you can or
you can't, you're right."

—Henry Ford

Consider a traffic accident. Every witness reports a different version of the same event; it can be difficult to figure out what really happened. In more personal conflicts and occurrences, it is even more confusing to find an objective reality. This is because every person drags the sum total of their history, sensitivities, and temperament into every situation and views everything through the filters of their own perception. Then they only allow themselves to see what fits into their belief system; they disallow what doesn't. As a friend of mine says, "I'll see it when I believe it!"

As human beings, we can't help but drag the past with us in the form of beliefs, which manifest in our expectations, our attitudes, our self-talk, and our behaviors. Many beliefs ("truths") that we hold are beyond our awareness. Yet, because beliefs exert a powerful influence on our day-to-day lives, a better life depends on making conscious choices about them.

From our earliest decisions, we created an internal map that helps us perceive, understand, and interpret the world. We use it all our lives—even long after it's outdated. Maps can be very helpful guides in reaching our destination, unless they are the wrong map! Imagine that, through a printing error, your map of Philadelphia was actually a map of Kansas City. No matter how hard you might study and work at it, you would still be confused and lost. Or imagine that your map was for the right city, but decades or centuries old. How well would you get around? It is important to update our internal maps and our deeply held truths and beliefs, so that we can trust them to guide us through the present and into the future.

An important part of the process of updating our maps is recognizing the fact that our personal "truths" are limited. As soon as we decide "that's the way it is!" we close doors to other possibilities. Our unconscious accepts anything we tell it as "truth" and works overtime to prove it again and again. Here are some of the self-defeating, incorrect "truths" we might tell ourselves:

"I'm no good." • "I deserve rejection." • "Life is pain." • "No one really loves me." • "I'm not good enough."• "There's something wrong with me." • "I don't fit in." • "If I love someone, I will be hurt." • "I'm a geek." • "I'm too fat." • "People can't be trusted." • "I'm not lovable." • "If people really knew me, they wouldn't like me."

With selective perception, we secretly look for data that proves that we are right. If I believe that I am unlovable, for example, I collect evidence to substantiate my beliefs. In doing that, I filter out—disallow—all data that doesn't fit what I hold to be true. And when it does fit I say, "Ah ha! That proves I was right." For better or worse, we keep reinforcing the behaviors that prove that we are right. And, unfortunately, we would so often rather be right than happy.

Exercises:

- Examine your earliest memories. What are the first decisions or "truths" you remember making about life?

- What do you believe about love? About children, authority, yourself — about God? Can you put those beliefs into words? Into writing?

- Spend time with your beliefs. Evaluate them. Jesus said, "It shall be done unto you as you believe." Do you want those things done unto you? If not, begin to dismantle them.

- Trace each "truth" to its source. Whose voice do you hear underneath the troublesome beliefs? Listen. Consider the possibility that they are not "true," but only one way of looking at things. Start poking holes in them. Or poking fun at them. What are some other interpretations?

- S-t-r-e-t-c-h your imagination; give someone else the benefit of the doubt. What is the best possible conclusion you might come up with? How might your life be different if you chose some different "truths"? Imagine, for instance, that you were and always have been lovable, that your parents really did love you fully for who you are. Play with this. Try it on for a day.

- Read a lot. Read philosophy, read fiction, read history, read poetry, read biographies. Get into other minds and other points of view. Learn from them.

Self-esteem is knowing that you are a worthwhile person. The higher your self-esteem, the more you will expect for and of yourself, and the more support you will give yourself toward attaining your goals. When you know that you're valuable and competent, you expect positive relationships and achievements, and you will probably manifest them. The lower your self-esteem, the lower your expectations. *In life, you generally get what you believe you deserve.*

"I've spent most of my life
confirming my preconceptions."
—Ashleigh Brilliant

Shame

"To say 'I love myself' can become your most powerful tool in healing the shame that binds you. To truly love yourself will transform your life."

—John Bradshaw

Shame is a deep, uncomfortable feeling that lurks at the edges of our every decision. It is connected to aspects of ourselves that are beyond our control; it is about who we are—being the wrong shape or color, being incompetent or stupid, not being good enough. Shame is not something that can easily be "fixed."

Shame is frequently instilled early in life with rebukes, ridicule, threats, shunning, and other forms of abuse and neglect. Many parents use shame as a way to control behavior and bring about conformity. They manipulate two of the most basic human needs: to belong to our primal family unit, and to be cherished for who we are.

Children, observing this treatment, believe they deserve it. They conclude that they are defective in some deep, unspeakable way. Having a need to idealize their parents because their very existence, survival, and place in the world depends on them, they tend to internalize judgments, and blame themselves for their own 'defectiveness.' This, of course, compounds the pain and complexity of the problem.

Repeated you-statements, such as "You're worthless," "You're bad," "Who do you think you are?" and the classic, "Shame on you!" can paralyze children. These statements judge, criticize, and blame. You-statements may be subtle, yet they can burrow very deep.

By contrast, if your parents told you, "I don't like what you *did*," they may have evoked a feeling of guilt, *specific* guilt, limited to the action. If you were able to fix the mistake, the guilt was—or should have been—released, and you learned judgment skills and wisdom. When, on the other hand, misbehavior was greeted with you-statements, you made a leap from *what you did* (specific behavior), to *who you are* (self-concept). "I did something stupid" becomes "I *am* stupid." "I made a mistake" becomes "I *am* a mistake." Or the behavior may have been corrected but the guilt not forgiven. The appropriate guilty feeling, relatively easy to correct and dissipate, may have worn a groove and become shame. The leap from *what I did* to *who I am* may have become even larger when the words "never" or "always" were tossed in. A simple word of guidance carelessly spoken can produce an avalanche of shame.

Both spoken and unspoken family rules such as "Don't talk back!" (or "Don't talk") and "Don't express your feelings" (or "Don't feel") compound the secrecy, confusion, and wounds. Covering up problems such as alcoholism, incest, or violence adds layers of shame and paralysis. A parent's personal shame can teach a child to be helpless.

The most important primal unit to which we belong, and which we need for our very survival, may splinter into antagonistic fragments in which parents and children are isolated in hopelessness and helplessness. When this happens, our primal need for love and acceptance goes unfilled.

With trust and communication skills absent, the only person we may be able to talk to is ourselves. And, of course, every single human being has a limited perspective. In our self-talk, therefore, we can replay the words of those important people and continue shaming ourselves. Or we might recognize the injustice and untruth of these judgments and turn our righteous anger outwards; or we can turn it inwards and take more than our fair share of the blame. We might give up any and all responsibility, distance ourselves from our families, and disown the parts of ourselves that desire their love. We may learn to protect ourselves from the pain, or learn to protect the "truth" we think we know: that we are unworthy. Covered up, hidden, buried from ourselves and others, shame can rear its ugly influence in a multitude of behaviors, both subtle and open, which are destructive to ourselves and/or to others.

If the primal source of shame, then, is our early experience with our parents, we must learn to champion ourselves against the messages that keep us helpless. If we can identify our primal wounds, we can give them the attention they need to heal. We need to do this so we can learn how not to inflict the same primal wounds on our own children and others we love. This is not easy. It is heroic work.

Nothing defends against the internal ravages of shame more than the security of the unconditional love of our parents or guardians, especially the sort of love that sees and appreciates us for what we are, respects our feelings, and accepts our differences and peculiarities. Nothing seems to create a more profound shame than the lack of that kind of love.

Shame is common to both men and women and there are similarities in how they deal with it. Both tend to cover it up with possessions, appearances, performance, and accomplishments. Both become "human doings" who do lots and lots of things to prove they are okay (though they themselves don't believe it), and to defend the wounded place deep inside. Current research identifies shame as an important element in aggression—including the violence of wife-beating—in addictions, obsessions, narcissism, depression, and numerous other psychiatric syndromes.

And there are differences in how men and women deal with shame. Women generally tend to turn their shame against themselves, punishing themselves for being immature, stupid, unattractive, unable to love, not able to "fit in." They try too hard and give too much, taking care of others without taking care of themselves. With their high depression rates from internalized self-hatred, women fill our mental hospitals.

Men's shame, on the other hand, derives more from weakness, incompetence, sexual inadequacy, and feelings of being needy and vulnerable. Men are socialized to be all things to all people, to be right and strong, to be dependable, responsible and independent, to be good providers, and to have all the answers. Anything that threatens this self-image, even making a mistake, can expose the shame and trigger rage. Men tend to act out this rage. They turn it against others, filling our prisons and jails.

Often feelings of shame are hard to identify, and may require a great deal of attention. Here are some ways you can begin to work through and unburden yourself of these darker feelings:

Exercises:

- Explore the source. Who or what judges you? Your mother? Your father? Peers? Who or what shamed you? Separate yourself from that source. Notice how *you* are still doing it to *yourself.*

- Question authority. As children, we needed and blindly accepted the guidance of all authorities. As adults, we need to question and discern which (if any) authority we will believe, trust, and follow, and to what extent. We have a choice.

- Champion yourself against shame. Identify and correct specific behaviors that are patterns of self-punishment. Resolve to stop punishing yourself. I have a friend who says, "When I spilled something, I used to say, 'That was stupid; I am so clumsy!' Now I say, 'That was silly.' It's not a judgment, just a comment."

- Put it into perspective. Your individual perceived failing or flaw is shared with thousands of others. You are not alone. Seek out friends, both in person and in books. Borrow wisdom and strategies for healing.

- Break the silence. Speak to safe, non-judging people in appropriate settings. Talk to a trusted friend, therapist, or support group. You might share a little, then check it out; if it's okay, you can tell a little more.

- Instead of talking yourself into feeling guilty and ashamed, talk yourself out of it! Listen closely to what you are saying to yourself. Then talk back to your self-talk!

- Laugh at your human-ness, your weaknesses. You might start with telling someone about some embarrassing moments.

- Lighten up. Get a different perspective. One woman, for example, gingerly told her support group that she was lesbian. The whole group responded with, "So what!"

- Write a family story. Remember something that happened which had a negative outcome. Reframe it and give it a wonderful ending.

- Talk to yourself as you would have liked your mom and dad to have talked to you. Give yourself the appreciation, respect, love, and support that you so desperately needed.

- Improve your communication skills so it becomes easier to talk with others.

- Develop supports for yourself. Find people you can talk to, feel safe with, and trust so that you can be who you really are and have fun together.

- Discover your sacred core. Your deepest self is holy, not profane. Reclaim the part of you that knows it is loving and lovable, whole and worthwhile, wise and wonderful.

When you were a child, you were not in control of life's events. Now, it is different. You can continue to recreate the past, as we do when we operate on automatic, or you can become conscious, take control of your life, and create a different future. The past need not become the future. The best place to begin is with a commitment to total self-honesty and self-support. Then examine and sort through what you inherited from society, parents, television, significant others, and church. Sift through and sort out the confusion. Unravel and release the knots that bind you.

Love Yourself

"I feel that all disease is ultimately related to
a lack of love, or to love that is only conditional,
for the exhaustion and depression of the immune
system thus created leads to physical vulnerability.
I also feel that all healing is related to the ability
to give and accept unconditional love."

—Dr. Bernie Siegel

Self-esteem depends on unconditional love: love with no strings attached; love with respect, acceptance, compassion, appreciation, empathy, and warmth; love that says, "Regardless of what you do, I love and accept you for who you are." I know a parent who told his child, "Even if you spend three years in kindergarten, I will still love you. I won't like it, but I will still love you."

Conditional love, on the other hand, is love that is turned off and on. It manipulates behavior by saying, "I love you *when*..., *because*..., or *if* you do what I want you to do." Some parents only show their love after a child has done something that pleases them. "I love you, honey, for cleaning your room!" Children who think they need to earn love become people pleasers, or perfectionists. Those who are raised on conditional love never really feel loved.

For some people, there seems to be a conflict between self-love and self-respect. Men, especially, who are taught to be more stoic with their feelings, may confuse self-love with self-indulgence, and close down to the nurturing "softness" of the idea. Self-love may seem to be a tricky line to walk between self-acceptance and strength of character.

According to the dictionary, respect means "holding in high regard." When you give yourself respect, you want to live up to yourself, with integrity. When you love yourself, you can then truly love others.

When you were born, you were totally and completely lovable. But maybe your parents couldn't see that. Maybe they didn't love themselves and, therefore, couldn't cherish you. Maybe they themselves had never been loved and were empty. Late in her life, my mother wondered, "How could I love when I was never loved?" She talked about how much she had always missed the love of her own mother. History, unfortunately, tends to repeat itself.

As a child I thought I was ugly. My parents never told me I was beautiful. Many years later my beautiful little daughter reminded me of old pictures of myself as a girl. I put two and two together, and eureka! If she's good looking, I must have been, too. If she's so lovable, I must have been, too. I took a second look at myself as a child, and felt some more old caterpillar beliefs start to crack and crumble. My childhood "truths" were simply not true.

If you weren't loved unconditionally when you were a child, you can now give that most precious gift to yourself. Tell yourself often, "I love myself totally and completely." Love heals people—those who give it and those who receive it. You are precious. You are lovable. Cherish yourself. You deserve it.

Exercises:

- Find some pictures of yourself as a baby. If you don't have one, use your imagination. Imagine your little self coming alive and moving. Look over your infant body with its tiny fingers and perfect fingernails; count your toes. Notice your rare and essential beauty, inside and out.

- Now, invite that child-self to come and sit on your lap. Enfold it in your arms. Invite it to speak to you. Listen. Listen. Esteem and cherish this child. Esteem and cherish this part of yourself.

- Imagine what you needed to hear many, many years ago. Whisper those words to your inner child. "You are beautiful. You have spectacular eyes." Tell this child, "I accept and love you totally and completely." Make a commitment to be best friends with your inner child to the end. Fill the hole in your soul with a total, no-strings-attached love for yourself—just the way you are.

The Golden Rule for Healing: "Do unto yourself what you wish your parents had done unto you." Now that you are an adult, you can give yourself the attention and compassion you may have missed out on: acceptance, respect, unconditional love, protection, understanding, appreciation. In re-parenting yourself, you can complete the unfinished business of your early years and heal the wounds. Every small change you make will have a ripple effect in the larger lake of your life. Before you know it, you will be emerging from your cocoon with the energy of the butterfly you once were.

Uncover and Reclaim Missing Parts

"The truth is that there is nothing within us that can hurt us; it is only our fear of experiencing our own feelings that can keep us trapped."

—Shakti Gawain

Every person has many different aspects of Self. Some are visible; others are not. It is important to take stock not only of the qualities we want the world to see, but also those which have been pushed into the background. The patterns of our daily lifestyles can force us into social roles we would not choose, for example, authoritarian boss, subservient secretary, bored production-line worker, overworked father, exhausted mother, reluctant baby-sitter, and so on. Often that is all others see in us, and after a while it may be difficult to remember all the other parts of who we are.

For wholeness, we need to uncover and recover the facets we have ignored, denied, and/or neglected. Healthy development demands that we have the courage to look at the entire picture and reclaim missing pieces. They may enrich our lives. We may discover or rediscover, for example, a long lost love of singing, writing, weaving, hiking, waltzing, playing cards, or debating politics. We need to find a place for these things in our lives.

When I was preparing for comprehensive exams for my doctorate several years ago, I was gripped with intense conflict. Sorting it out, I realized that the "don't be smart" messages of my childhood were rearing up to sabotage me. Over the years I had not been encouraged to develop or be proud of my intellectual capabilities. Only after much anguish was I able to reframe my thinking. I affirmed that it is okay and good to be smart and that I am smart. The conflict subsided. I took my comps and passed!

Many women have been taught to deny or downplay their intelligence and the strong qualities that might be "unfeminine" and intimidate men. Many men have been taught to deny and devalue "soft" qualities, feelings of gentleness and sensitivity, for example, which they think may make them less "masculine." Yet the source of personal transformation is often through parts of ourselves which have been denied, neglected, or closed off to our awareness.

It can be scary to explore the unknown. Yet keeping parts of ourselves hidden ultimately drains our energy and creativity, and is a loss of potential. A rather easy way to tap new sources of energy, therefore, is simply to reframe and reclaim existing energy in new ways. We may uncover unexpected treasures. In this personal spring cleaning, we may also discover items we have outgrown and which are no longer of use.

Exercises:

- List some of your characteristics as a child. Were you trusting, athletic, inquisitive, smart, tenacious, artistic, honest, playful, emotional, musical, eager to learn? What were you good at? What did that look like?

- Remember the response of your parents to each quality. Which did they appreciate and encourage? Which did they discourage? Look at each quality as if you were your own accepting, adoring mom or dad.

- You can now choose what to do with it, how to express it, suppress it, or channel it as it fits in your life. Which areas do you want to attend to, develop, or change? How might you go about doing it? For example, I love to go dancing yet seldom did it. So I got a list of all the dance groups in town. Now I go dancing several times a month.

Be aware of the different parts of yourself and the many hats you wear. Like pieces in a puzzle, each facet belongs to you. And every restored part is a move closer to integrity, harmony, and health.

All or Nothing Thinking

"Breasts come in two sizes: too big and too small."

—Anonymous

"Either I'm perfect or I'm a complete failure." "Either I don't trust at all, or I trust too much." "Either I'm feeling terrific, or I'm terrible." "Either I don't need anyone, or I need him so much that I can't live without him." "Either I'm totally responsible or totally irresponsible." This extreme "pits or peaks" thinking is all too familiar for children from troubled families.

Everything is either black or white, with no in-between. Things are either all right or all wrong. This all-or-nothing thinking creates anxiety, destroys serenity, and plays havoc with self-esteem.

Most people experience occasional periods of time when life is not as it should be and everything does seem awful. Yet, like a summer storm, these times pass quickly and freshen the air. Like the weather, many factors influence our moods, our energy, and our attitudes. Sunlight or lack thereof, barometric pressure, raging hormones, and personal bio-rhythms can throw us off balance and also can bring richness. Then, balance is regained and life goes on. Yet, either-or thinking causes more trouble than any of these natural influences.

I once asked a returning Peace Corps physician about the landscape in the Middle East. With a twinkle in his eye he told me that he had learned to appreciate subtle shades of brown. As we learn to distinguish and appreciate the many subtle shades of brown and gray in our personal lives, we will find more enjoyment and peace.

Exercises:

- Watch for the extremes in your thinking. Do you flip between "Everything is wonderful" and "Everything is awful?" Are things either a "Perfect Ten" or a "Big Zero?" Identify what you do and write about it in your journal.

- Now, write one "peak" sentence (Perfect Ten) on the top of a page and the corresponding "pit" sentence (Big Zero) on the bottom and try to fill in the 9, 8, 7, 6, 5, 4, 3, 2, and 1. If, for instance, you wrote, "Everything's gone wrong," as the "0." list some things that have not gone wrong. Stretch your imagination to see how many ideas you can come up with to develop your gray scale.

Dualism (either/or thinking) is a construct of the mind. It polarizes opposites. Instead, think in circles; with both/and thinking, you can see the connections between black and white, and gain insight into their relationship. Without two sides, a coin is worthless.

Stress Relief

"We are asking ourselves what is real, what is honest, what is quality, what is valued, what is really important."

—Faith Popcorn, futurist

A multitude of stress-related and immune system diseases have cropped up in this century. The pace of life in the late twentieth century has quickened to break-neck speed. Life in the fast lane is overwhelming and exhausting, and results in stress which is unhealthy for all living creatures. With so much time pressure and intense anxiety, there is little room left over for play and laughter, family and friends, and the other things that make life worthwhile.

God's tenth commandment was "remember the Sabbath and keep it holy." *Sabbath*, from which we derive our word Saturday, comes from the Hebrew word *Shabbat*, meaning, "to sit." We have forgotten how to sit, just sit, and keep our minds on higher things.

When I was a child, Sunday was the traditional day of rest; it would start with the family going to church together. When supermarkets first intended to be open on Sundays, the women in the church picketed in protest. At first sales were slow on Sundays, until the stores began running specials in order to entice people in on their day of rest. Over time, this practice has brought about dramatic changes in our society—which we have come to accept as normal. The one day in the week designated for rest and recreation is, to most Americans, as busy and hectic as the rest of the week.

Relaxation, these days, can be just as stressful as work. It may entail complicated and expensive gear, hectic vacations, careful planning, and a hundred details. It can mean spending hours on crowded freeways. It can mean spending lots of time and money on carefully engineered media experiences such as movies and amusement parks. Days of real rest and relaxation are all too rare.

Exercises:

- Simplify your life to reduce the stressors and relieve the time and financial pressures. In your job, your home life, and your relationships, remember the K.I.S.S. motto: Keep It Simple, Sweetie.

- Spend time alone daily. Just a five minute pause can make a difference. Take several mini vacations during the day. You might reminisce or imagine being on a cruise or on a lovely tropical island. Learn other relaxation techniques.

- Get enough sleep. Your body needs it.

- Live one day at a time. Most anxiety lives either in the past or in the future, in worries about what has already occurred or worries about what might happen. Living in the present reduces stress.

- Give up being a superperson. Lower unrealistic expectations of yourself. Try to avoid things that increase your stress levels.

- Play more. Put more fun and laughter in your life. Exercise and enjoy your body. Spend unstructured time with friends, and see what happens.

- Get a rocker or swing for your porch. Use it regularly.

Breathe

"In English, to inhale is to inspire—to take in the spirit. To exhale, or expire, means to release the spirit. All of life can be observed as a taking in, and a giving out of movement and rest, of controlling and letting go."
—Regina Sara Ryan and John W. Travis, M.D.

A guitarist friend of mine observed her living-room audience and commented, "You can tell who is from a dysfunctional family—the ones who aren't breathing!" Emotions are closely connected to breathing. If our breathing is generally shallow, we may be stuffing our feelings. When we breathe, feelings flow through us like the wind in the trees.

Take a few deep, controlled breaths right now. Inhale. Exhale. Repeat. Notice what happens. As breathing deepens, stress is reduced; conversely, as stress is reduced, breathing tends to deepen.

As stress goes up, breathing becomes shallow and peace of mind and self-esteem suffer. The body, endangered from without or by disturbing thoughts from within, reacts to protect itself. The resulting fight-or-flight response triggers a set of automatic responses that affect the heart rate, the flow of blood to the muscles, and the rate of breathing. Oxygen serves a life-giving function for the body, bringing vitality to every cell. When breathing is restricted or suppressed, the body does not receive the oxygen it requires to carry out necessary functions. Irritation, sleepiness, headaches, or more serious symptoms may ensue.

When young children conclude that the world is unsafe, they may hold their breath to control their feelings and to numb their fear. Many continue to constrict their breathing, to try and brace themselves against the fears and risks of living life fully.

Eastern medicine and all subtle energy practices are based on systems of chi. Chi, or prana, is the life force that we gather when we breathe. Do you know someone who seems to have more energy than anyone you know? Pay attention to their breathing.

The more aware people are of their breathing, the greater access they have to their own life energy. When we are not breathing deeply, our minds can fill with noise, chatter, and worry, which can affect us negatively. Feelings get stuck. As a result, we are less effective and don't enjoy ourselves as much.

Exercises:

- Exercise! Get plenty of brisk exercise at least every other day. Select an activity that helps you to breathe fully and replenish the oxygen supply throughout your body. Walking is excellent.

- Let go of stress by controlling your breathing. Sit up straight and focus on your breath for a few minutes. As you inhale think, "I am..." As you exhale think, "...relaxed." Continue with your eyes closed. You can also inhale to the count of ten and exhale to the count of ten. Do this for five or ten minutes; you'll feel completely refreshed.

- Put your hand on your chest, and fill your lungs up all the way. Now exhale completely. Put your other hand on your abdomen. Inhale again, filling your belly so that it moves when you have your hand. Exhale. Now fill up your lungs and your belly. Exhale. This is a deep breath, which fills every minute alveolus, and you have hundreds of billions of them. When you exhale, remember to release all the air you possibly can, to clean out the old air in every corner of your lungs.

✻   ✻   ✻

As caterpillars cast off the layers that constrict them, new colors and patterns emerge indicating that metamorphosis is in progress. Like peeling off a too-tight sweater, the uncomfortable process leaves more room to breathe. For us humans, it's the same. As we cast off the layers that have hindered our development and stunted our growth, new behaviors emerge to signal that metamorphosis is in progress.

It takes time and courage to examine outdated beliefs, judgments, opinions, and perceptions—and all the evidence we've collected to prove them to ourselves. Metamorphosis calls for a reweaving of the fabric of our lives. We need to examine the threads that have tripped up our self-confidence, crippled our self-worth, and strangled our creativity. We need to notice the troublesome patterns and unravel the knots. What has been learned can be unlearned. It's time to release the thoughts and behaviors that don't work and learn what will help us to thrive in the world.

This is not easy for us humans who have layer upon layer of history that has been fastidiously collected and carefully treasured. But we have the power to change. There is always another chance to get rid of what we don't want and replace it with what we do want.

It calls for a willingness and a commitment to be completely honest with yourself. It calls for the courage to learn new skills, to see with new eyes, and to move on to a new relationship with yourself, with others, and with life. As you grow and let go, you become the beautiful person you were meant to be.

7

REACHING OUT

*"When one is a stranger to oneself then one is
estranged from others, too. If one is out of touch
with oneself, then one cannot touch others....
Only when one is connected to one's own core
is one connected to others."*

—Anne Morrow Lindbergh

EVERYTHING IN the universe is connected to everything else. It's no mystical secret that as your esteem for yourself goes up, so does your esteem for others and likewise their esteem for you. By understanding and accepting yourself, you gain insight into—and compassion for—your fellow men, women, and children. These changes can have a ripple effect and spread into your entire community. Every healthy relationship you nurture moves you farther away from unhealthy patterns. No matter whom this relationship is with, your future relationships will be better for it...and so will you. This chapter is about ways of connecting with others—things a "social butterfly" does.

Trust

*"I think we may safely trust
a good deal more than we do."*

—Henry David Thoreau

I ask my workshop participants to complete the sentence, "Trust is...." No matter where I go, I hear the same definitions. Trust is an act of faith, belief in the other, honesty, confidence, predictability, absence of fear, willingness to be vulnerable, ability to let go, feeling safe, and the basis for security and intimacy. Then I ask, "On a scale from one to ten, how important is trust to you?" I begin to count, watching for hands to appear. No matter where I speak, when I get to "ten," a roomful of hands waves at me. The greater the trust, the less people need to be fearful, withdrawing, or on guard. For basic reasons, trust is crucial.

Whom do we trust in life? People who are trustworthy! The more worthy of trust they are, the greater the likelihood of our risking openness with them. This works both ways. When we are perceived to be trustworthy, others will be more likely to be honest and open with us. Trust-building is a two way street. When trust occurs, a ground of safety exists in which stories (and feelings) can unfold and personalities can blossom.

I was brought up on a philosophy that people are inherently sinful, fundamentally bad. Believing that also about myself, I didn't trust my wants or needs or intuition; I fought myself constantly, and always felt like I was swimming against the current. Nor did I trust others. For me, human nature itself was suspect.

In graduate school I learned, to my surprise, that human nature is not generally inclined toward evil; rather, it is either neutral or tends toward goodness. After this realization, I began to work on building my own trust for myself, bit by bit, and also let myself trust a few select others, people who eventually became my friends.

Trust is not an either-or arrangement, but builds in increments. You share a bit, then check it out; if it seems okay, you can share some more. Give others a chance, perhaps in small increments at first. Choose to be a little more trusting.

Learn to trust your body, your intuition, your judgments. Part of this process involves identifying the situations in which you don't trust yourself (around chocolate, perhaps, or in certain romantic situations, or with credit cards). Then take steps to become more trustworthy for yourself, and also for your children and your friends. This is not easy for persons from dysfunctional families, but it is essential for health and happiness. In doing this you will create an environment where safety and honesty, love and connectedness can flourish.

Exercises:

- Meet the needs of the child within you (your "inner child"), your "outer" children, if you have any, and your adult self.

- Think of all the people you trust in your life. Why do you trust them? How far and in what circumstances do you trust them?

- Here are other ways to increase the trust in relationships:

  - Accept and respect other people for *who they are.*

  - Honor differences, and learn to enjoy other perspectives.

  - Treat others with the same respect and caring that you like to have.

  - Spend comfortable, quality time together. Be there for them.

  - Say what you mean—with tact. Don't give insincere praise.

  - Respect boundaries. Respect their privacy. Keep secrets.

  - Let them know they can count on you.

Trust is a choice. When I worry because my daughter leaves her car unlocked, travels alone, or talks to strangers, she reassures me: "I choose to trust people." Rarely is she let down, and her life is much lighter and richer for it.

Play More

"If you can walk you can dance.
If you can talk you can sing."

—saying from Zimbabwe

Growing up with abuse, neglect, addiction, and other trauma is very, very serious business. From early on we learn not to be ourselves, but rather to be whatever and whoever it takes to be safe. The struggle to survive childhood prevents healthy growth and development.

Kids from unhealthy families have had to take things far too seriously in their lives, and have missed out on the better parts of childhood. But it's not too late to get in on the fun! Life is, in fact, a laughing matter. When you laugh and play, self-esteem goes up, stress goes down, and love just happens. Laugher can heal body and soul.

The well-known writer, Norman Cousins, was diagnosed with a chronic debilitating disease. Refusing to believe that he would only get worse, then die, he decided to do anything and everything he could to defeat the disease process. He chose good humor as part of his cure and filled his hospital room with laughter. Over time, he succeeded in regaining perfect health. Imagine what a little levity might do for you.

The universal language of play is one of the healthiest things in any culture. When we play we ignite the original spark of creativity within ourselves, the spark that represents our truest selves. With play we allow ourselves to give and accept spontaneous gifts of joy. When we are relaxed, we open ourselves to insight on our situations. When we have fun, vitality and *joie de vivre* pervade our entire being.

The next time you hear that voice inside telling you to keep your mouth shut and your clothes clean; don't be silly, and don't laugh... question it. The word "silly" is not a four-letter word. In fact, it comes from the German root "selig," which means *blessed*.

Exercises:

- Look for the light side of things. Laugh more—at yourself and with others. A regular dose of giggles and snorts does wonderful—even astonishing—things for your emotional and physical health and well-being.

- Ask kids if you can play with them. Kids are born with inner joy. Play is as natural to them as breathing. They'll tell you what to do. Relax with them and let your interactions stir dormant parts of yourself—the mystical butterfly parts—and bring aliveness, spontaneity, and joy into the moment.

- After you put this book down, do one of the following: climb a tree; skip down the sidewalk; be a clown; make a face in the mirror; say "I love you" to a teddy bear; look for things that tickle your funny bone; laugh until your sides hurt; pretend; dress in a costume; be outrageous!

- Make fun time a high priority today and every day.

Learn to Really Listen

"God gave us two eyes, two ears and only one mouth. Use them in this ratio."

—Anonymous

Most people think they are good listeners, yet few really are. Good listening keeps us healthy and happy and helps us discover that we have stories to tell.

Good listeners take the time to be there for their family and friends. They put themselves aside and get into the other's shoes. This quality of attention says, "You are important and interesting and are worth listening to." Their self-esteem then moves up a few notches.

Exercises:

Invite someone to tell you a story so you can practice active listening:

- Look interested, and be interested. What is your body language saying to the speaker? Try leaning forward, looking them in their eyes. Does this put them at ease? Does it increase their enthusiasm for talking to you?

- Put aside judgment and criticism. It erodes communication. Remember what it has done to your own stories.

- Notice the speaker's non-verbal cues, such as gulping, sighing, inflection, and posture. All these things add to the story.

- Ask questions to draw the speaker out further, if you like. "And then what?" "What was that like?" "How were you feeling?"

- Open up to understand their feelings. What would you have felt had this happened to you? This ability to share the same feeling is the essence of empathy.

- Let them finish their story. It's often difficult not to jump in and tell our own stories. But hold off. Don't interrupt. Bite your tongue. You'll get your turn.

- Finally, reflect back this feeling. "You must have been excited...," "I bet you were scared when...." Allow them to correct you, if necessary, until you reach an understanding.

If you listened well and reflected accurately, the speaker will probably breathe a sigh of relief at being understood, or perhaps exclaim with excitement, "Yes, you're right!" They will also think you are very bright and interesting. Good listening skills are as difficult to learn as driving a car. They may feel awkward at first. But with practice they soon become second nature.

Let Go of Comparison

"Always be a first-rate version of yourself instead of being a second-rate version of someone else."

—Judy Garland to her daughter, Liza Minelli

I used to compare my insides to everyone else's outsides. It's easy to see in others the desirable qualities that we wish we had ourselves. If we use our comparisons to better ourselves, and to discover aspects of ourselves we did not know existed, they are used well. However, if we use comparison to judge ourselves (or others) harshly, it damages our self-esteem and creates anguish in our lives.

Do you compare yourself to others? How many? How often? Think about what you do when you compare yourself. Generally people find the best quality in everyone else, compare themselves unfavorably, and feel inadequate and inferior; then they beat themselves up and put themselves down. Comparison sets us up for unhealthy competition. It drives wedges between people, creates separation, and enforces conformity.

There are always people who are "better" or "worse" at something than you are. When you compare yourself, you either feel smug or guilty. It is a very popular game with temporary, shallow rewards or lasting, deep consequences. Comparison is a very poor measure of your real worth.

Exercises:

- You are unique. You are one of a kind. It's not fair, therefore, to judge yourself by anyone else's standards. Set or choose your own. Compare yourself only to yourself.
- Celebrate your uniqueness. Go for your own personal best. Express your individuality, your personality.
- You can strengthen the qualities you like in yourself by looking for them in others. Enjoy and celebrate them.
- Keep competition where it belongs: on the game field, where all the rules are up front. Competition can help us to better ourselves when it is seen as an opportunity, and not a judgment.

When we realize that we are not adversaries to everyone, that we really are all in this together, we can create relationships and families based on cooperation and harmony. In doing this we need to let go of "win-lose" thinking. We can design "win-win" situations, where everyone's needs are met, and everyone's successes are valued and appreciated.

Consider others as models who can show you new possibilities. Instead of putting yourself down, use what you like in others to lift yourself up. For example, if you think Jane is a great cook, don't be jealous; instead, ask her for a recipe. Change your self-talk.

Seeing with fresh eyes, we will find people everywhere who can inspire us to new heights. Even children can be our models. I've learned some of my most important lessons from my kids.

Forgive and Forget

"Forgiveness is the ultimate preventative medicine as well as the greatest healer."

—Marianne Williamson

We have all been hurt by the mistakes of key adults in our lives. And we have hurt others. Blame and resentment trap us in the past, and victimize us in the present. Forgiveness, on the other hand, sets us free from the prison of pain that was undeserved.

Forgiveness does not excuse behaviors. It does not mean approval. Rather, it involves a willingness to see with compassion. Forgiveness means that you've decided to deal with the negative feelings, put them behind you, and move on. The person who hurt you probably did what he did out of his own weakness and shortcomings. You did not deserve it. Now you can make the decision to let go of the chains that bind you—and put them to rest forever.

For half a century my relationship with my mother had been filled with conflict. Over the years I'd attempted and worked toward healing and understanding, with little success. A grown woman with grown children of my own, I attended a workshop where we did an exercise on forgiveness. I realized that I wanted to "let her off the hook" totally and completely.

The next day I visited my eighty-eight-year old mother in her nursing home. "Mother, we need to talk." She listened passively, slumped in a wheelchair. Awkwardly I admitted my part in it. "I know that I was a difficult child for you." I apologized for the pain I had caused her. I told her that she did an okay job as a parent and that I was okay. Eyes closed, she was fading in and out; I wasn't sure she was hearing me. I continued, thanking her for the good things she had done for me, and listed a few of them (cooking good food, letting me go to college, etc.). Then I said "I love you," and meant it fully. I paused, feeling complete. Silence filled the room. I asked her if she had anything she wanted to say to me. After a long pause she said, "Forgive me."

Those were her last words to me. She died three days later. Perhaps that forgiveness was what she had been waiting for.

Forgiveness is an act, not a long process. With forgiveness we shed the caterpillar layers of the past and heal our memory and ourselves. Lightening our burden, we lighten our journey, and get the metamorphosis moving in the right direction.

Exercises:

- Write the name of a person who has injured you at the top of a piece of paper. Then list their transgressions. Spend as much time as necessary doing this.

- Ask yourself if you are ready to let go of this burden. Have you carried it around long enough? Are you willing to let them off the hook? Are you willing to forgive them?

- Shred or burn the paper.

If you are guilty of some wrong, it is your duty to right it, to clean it up. Here are some tips:

- Make a list of some people you have harmed or injured. Find out if they were indeed harmed by your words or actions. You may be taking it too seriously. Or not seriously enough. Ask forgiveness. Ask them how you can make it up to them. Find a way to pay off your debts.

- Forgive yourself and let it go. Sometimes you cannot or do not need to make amends.

- Don't blame yourself for things that were out of your control. You probably did the best you could, given the information you had at the time.

- Learn from your mistakes. They are your teachers. There are lessons in every one of them. Figure out how you can do it differently next time.

Reach Out and Connect

"When you have an interaction, huge new regions of yourself bubble up from within."

—Brian Swimme

High school years were good ones for me. I liked my all-girls' school, was involved in the orchestra and choir, and my self-esteem was at a peak. A club to which I belonged had wiener roasts and pajama parties and was lots of fun. With graduation, however, everything changed.

Weddings, college, and the work force quickly dissolved our club, and the most important supports in my young adult life vanished. In the 60s, husband and wife were supposed to be all things to each other; all other social supports, therefore, frequently withered. Once married and settled in the suburbs, I felt that friendships with women were somehow subversive and friendships with men were threatening to my primary relationship. This severely restricted my options and set me up for painful isolation in my all-American nuclear suburban family, estranged from everyone except my husband and three children.

One dysfunctional part of our society seems only to value and encourage sexual relationships between men and women; all other caring supports and connections are suspect. We have been divided from others in countless ways. With comparison and competition, racism, sexism, and homophobia, people have learned to be adversaries, to be against each other. Crucial communication skills are often not learned. As a result, the searing pain of loneliness is all too common for children and teenagers, single and married adults, parents and grandparents alike.

We need people in our lives—people who like to talk and listen to us, who sustain us, who bring us joy. Every individual needs others to meet basic human needs and to help them survive and thrive. No healthy man, woman, or child is an island.

A Chilean woman once told me that in her country friendships are passed down from one generation to the next; the grandparents of different families are friends, as are the parents, and the children. After living here for many years she concluded, "In America, everyone is your friend and no one is your friend."

Divide and conquer is an ancient strategy for controlling people that has long been used around the world and in our society. We have been fragmented from family and friends, from our ethnic roots, from our neighborhoods and communities, from nature. In the name of individuality, competition, and progress, we separate ourselves from others whose well-being we believe somehow threatens our own. We move constantly, and most of us live with deep feelings of alienation, disconnection, and loneliness.

Yet, throughout the centuries and around the world, women have traditionally come together over common tasks such as tending children, making and preserving food, sewing quilts and clothing, and supervising the marketplaces. They have gathered for life passages such as childbirth, marriage, and sending the dead on their way. Women found a shared strength in these gatherings, and their broad support base and social contact enriched them and their families. They depended on each other for their survival, helping each other and being helped when they needed it.

Historically, men have also had important alliances and friendships with each other. They gathered in rural communities and in urban workplaces, in war councils and sporting events, in clubs and pubs. And for hundreds of generations, extended families provided a framework for belonging, survival, and support.

After the turn of the century, more and more Americans began to migrate to cities and live independently. Rural community living and multi-generational families became less the norm than nuclear urban and suburban families. Today, a larger proportion of American families have few or no children, and there are increasing numbers of single-person households. Individuals are more isolated. Time and work pressures put a squeeze on family and friendships. Therefore, with smaller, far-flung families, we need to find or design meaningful connections. We have to work harder to extend our support base and build deep human bonds both within our families and beyond them.

Exercises:

- Make a list of the most important people in your life. Do they know how important they are to you? When is the last time you called or wrote them? (A form letter is better than no letter at all.)

- Time heals many wounds. If you had a bad ending to a very special relationship, you may want to contact that person to see if they're open to meeting. Getting together, talking, and forgiving can heal your past and future relationships.

- Reach out and trade phone numbers with one new person this week. Call him or her within a few days to plan to do something together.

- Make time for friends a priority in your schedule. Find a common interest with people important to you. A regular meeting or activity lays the foundation for friendships to grow. Consider lunch dates, regular hikes, video nights, monthly potluck dinners.

- Do fun things together. Play! Find companions to discover new things with. Go to the zoo, movies, shows, races, dances. There are hundreds of ways to make friends.

- Improve your communication skills. Walks can provide an opportunity for easy conversation; discussion groups can be more focused.

- Create celebrations for birthdays and rituals for special occasions. Plan parties, dinners, annual backpacking or ski outings or holiday gatherings. Bring together the favorite people in your life.

Setting Boundaries

"Good fences make good neighbors."

—Robert Frost

When a person decides to shed some old behaviors and learn new ones, everything begins to shift. Some relationships will crumble, and others will become healthier. And like the metamorphosis of a caterpillar, once you begin, there's no turning back.

Personal boundaries have to do with the setting of limits. Boundaries help us define our identity and determine our destiny. We need to decide who we are, what we believe, what we expect—and what we will not tolerate. This set of spoken and unspoken rules regulates how people treat one another.

Our personal rules spring from our awareness of personal rights and reflect our self-respect and self-esteem—what we believe we deserve for ourselves. We teach others how to treat us (no phone calls after 10 P.M., for example). As a matter of fact, people often respect you more when you set boundaries, because it encourages them to be more self-aware as well.

The lower our self-esteem, the more we'll settle for what we don't want, believing that we don't deserve better. The higher our self-esteem, on the other hand, the more we believe we deserve good things in life. And the higher our expectations for our lives, the better prepared we are to accept the good things and reject the bad things when they happen.

Like riding a bicycle, we need skills to go forward and skills to stop. We need to know how to turn away from what we don't want, and toward what we do want. This implies that you are riding your bike, and not being taken for a ride. You are in charge of figuring out what you want and where you will go. You will probably take many wrong turns, even a few dead ends; but each one can bring you closer to discovering what you do want. When the road gets rough or starts to head into places you don't want to visit, you can turn around. When people get too close or don't respect you, your intuition will tell you. Listen to that voice. Then teach people how to treat you.

The instinct for boundary-setting comes naturally to children Without being taught, toddlers say, "Stop that!" or "I don't like that." Many parents, however, don't like children speaking up for themselves in this way, and extinguish this behavior. These same children, then, as adults, have to take assertiveness classes to relearn what they once knew naturally. Problems can also occur when parents do not set boundaries for themselves, and allow children to run their lives.

Parents can either encourage or discourage healthy boundary setting in families. With my own two babies eleven months apart, I watched my son take away every toy that my daughter was playing with. She would cry and cry. So I laid on the floor beside her, wrapped my hands over the little fingers that clutched the toy, and taught her to say, "No!" In her first assertiveness lesson at thirteen months of age, she began to learn that she had rights and had to stick up for them.

As children, we needed our parents to protect us, to be responsible for us, and to set limits for us. As we got older, we needed our parents to guide us and teach us how to do those things for ourselves. If this happened to you, if you were taught to expect respect and to stand up for your rights, you were most fortunate.

If our parents had overly rigid structure and rules ("Children should be seen and not heard," for example) we may have felt stifled. We may have learned that what we want is unimportant and doesn't matter. We may have concluded that we also didn't matter.

Those who grew up, on the other hand, with unclear or enmeshed boundaries, grew up with confusion, not knowing what they liked or wanted, not knowing their rights or responsibilities; everyone was responsible for everyone else's problems. "You don't know what you want," may have added to the confusion. With the blurring of boundaries, they didn't know where one person started and another ended. People with enmeshed boundaries may think they "own" or "belong to" each other; they don't realize, though, that although they may share a bond with others, they belong only to themselves.

Boundaries help people form their identity and become autonomous, whole persons. Separate boundaries can be set for the body, feelings, ideas, needs, wants and/or beliefs. Boundaries spring from the knowledge that we deserve respect, that we have rights, and that we can decide the rules for our own life.

Like a mobile with many objects hanging interdependently in balance with one another, change in one affects and brings about corresponding changes in others. If you are single, establishing boundaries is easier to do. Others tend to be less affected and less reactive to your changes. In a relationship or a family, your changes make more of a difference.

Whether or not you are in a relationship, try to engage the support of the most important people in your life. If they resist your changes, if they don't want to change themselves, figure out how to deal with and move through the resistance. Filling in developmental holes—playing "catch-up"—in adulthood may be awkward for everyone. It will get easier with support, with practice, and with time.

Exercises:

- Make a list of the things you don't like and don't want from others. Now, turn the paper over and list what you do like and do want.

- People are not mind readers. Once you have determined what you like and expect from other people, let them know. Encourage and reward the behavior you do want with your attention and appreciation.

- Once you have become clear about behavior you will not accept from others, tell them, tactfully. A good start is to "just say no," or, "no, thanks." Be kind. You don't have to be mean to mean business.

- Learn to ask for what you want. This one little trick makes life so much easier!

- Ask permission before you cross another's boundaries. For example, asking "Is it okay if I give you a hug?" respectfully checks out the desires of the other. Without permission, a hug can feel like an invasion.

- Take an assertiveness class if you need more guidance or practice.

As you determine what you don't like and don't want, notice also how important it is for you. Is it important enough to make an issue, or small enough to overlook? Use your good judgment.

Boundaries have a fluidity. They change depending on who we are dealing with, and what the trust level is. As people and life change, allow your boundaries to do the same.

Responsibility—Yours, Mine, and Ours

"To the question of your life, you are the only answer.
To the problems of your life, you are the only solution."

—Jo Coudert

Responsibility means being willing and able to respond. When you were born, your parents had total responsibility for your care and well-being. You were helpless and unable to be responsible. As you became older and more capable, your responsibility increased and theirs decreased.

Your long range developmental task in life is to shift from having no responsibility as an infant to having total responsibility for yourself as an adult. If this transfer did not occur, your parents carried more responsibility than was necessary. If they did for you what you should have done for yourself, they deprived you of your own *self-responsibility*. If, on the other hand, they exercised too little responsibility, you had to carry too much. Either of those situations may cause you difficulties as an adult.

Problems arise when we exercise either too much or too little responsibility. For example, if I evade responsibility for myself, my children (if I have any), or my work, I am being neglectful. Avoidance of personal responsibility ("there's nothing I can do") can lead to a sense of helplessness and powerlessness.

People raised in alcoholic homes are often overly responsible. If I overdo responsibility, if I try to manipulate and control others, they don't like it and get angry. Blame, fault-finding, and guilt can fly and self-esteem suffers. If I assume responsibility for other's feelings and behaviors, it confuses boundaries. When communication skills are lacking and people don't ask or don't say "no," family members have to be hyper-vigilant and second-guess each other.

I was once speaking on the phone to someone on a car phone. As we were talking, she was pulled over for speeding. Over 1,500 miles away, I felt a pang of guilt! I worked to sort it out. She was the one behind the wheel, not me. But even though I was in no way responsible, I was relieved to learn that she didn't get a ticket.

Now that you are captain of your own ship, you can decide how and where to go. You are responsible for your feelings. You are responsible for your decisions and choices. You are responsible for your actions and the consequences. Enjoy the freedom and empowerment that are your just reward.

Exercises:

- Let go of blame. It is an expression of powerlessness which creates more powerlessness and negativity in the world. Think, instead, in terms of responsibility, and get on with resolving the problem.

- The next time something goes wrong, write out the story. Then write it again, with a different, and better, ending.

- Sort out what's yours, theirs, and what you share. Who owns the problem? Distinguish between what is in your domain of responsibility, what isn't.

- Trust more and stop trying to control all outcomes. I once realized that the more I trusted, the less I "needed" to be in control; it also works the other way round. Contrary to popular opinion, it is not your responsibility to solve every problem or handle every situation. Sometimes you just need to get out of the way. A friend once observed, "The more I let go, the better it gets."

- There are always things beyond your control, big things like the economy, political situations, pollution, and other problems that are created by many people together. These are not your fault; don't blame yourself for them. You may not have any control over these things, but you can control your own response and your attitude toward them, and may ultimately have more power to improve those situations than you think.

Notice Connections

"In all of life, there are sequential stages of growth
and development. A child learns to turn over,
to sit up, to crawl, and then to walk and run.
Each step is important and each one takes time.
No step can be skipped."

—Stephen R. Covey

Around the world and for hundreds of generations, people have learned about life from life itself. "As you sow, so shall you reap." "What goes around, comes around." "Every action has an equal and opposite reaction." They learned about the process of life—that there is a natural sequence of events that takes time.

When we understand and work with Mother Nature, there is a positive consequence, such as an abundant harvest. On the other hand, ignoring, violating, or trying to shortcut the process can result only in frustration and disappointment. If, for example, you plant corn too early or too late, there will be no harvest. An impatient caterpillar that pastes on wings is doomed to fall when it tries to fly.

In rural settings, we can see connections clearly. If this..., then that.... The action-reaction cycle is obvious. One man told me that, as a boy, he forgot to feed the pigs and turkeys; the next day he "nearly got trampled to death because they were so hungry." He clearly saw the consequence of his behaviors and learned the lesson. If he didn't learn from that situation and again missed a feeding, the same consequence would result to again teach him the lesson.

In our technological society, in which most people are disconnected from the land, we can miss out on the important lessons of process and natural change. We can miss out on noticing the relationships between what we think and how we feel, between what we say and how others feel, between what we do and what it brings to us, to others, and to the earth.

Exercises:

- It's tempting to see life as a series of unrelated and uncontrollable events. But look for connections in your life. Take a step back to examine what's happening to you now. Review the sequence of choices that brought you to where you are. What actions have you taken in the past whose consequences still affect you today?

- Notice connections in your relationships. When, for example, you see certain emotions on a person's face, try to back up to figure out what words, events, or experience put them there.

- Observe inner connections. When your self-esteem sags, back up and review your thoughts, your words, your behaviors, your self-care (or lack of it).

- Notice that "what goes around, comes around." How you treat others affects how they treat you. The people whose judgment we most fear may be the very persons we ourselves are criticizing and judging the most. On the other hand, our best relationships may have happened because of the positive time and energy we have invested in them.

- Everything in interconnected. We breathe the same air as everyone else on the planet, and our destiny is intricately interrelated. Countless irresponsible and reckless actions, such as dumping nuclear wastes, all have serious consequences. The more we see and understand the connections, the more we will gain the wisdom, the insight, and the courage to take action and avert disaster.

Reaching out and connecting with others brings a sense of well-being and support. Living by principles of respect and integrity may not make you a social butterfly, but they will help you fly.

REACHING HIGH

*"I say unto you: a man must have chaos yet within
him to be able to give birth to a dancing star."*

—Nietzche

ALWAYS IN a state of flux, self-esteem must be maintained, like a household, like a diet, like a bank account, like a garden. Putting your choices into action is the key to living life fully. In learning to master your thoughts and emotions, your addictions, your passions, and your desires, life becomes less of a struggle, and more of a dance.

And yet, living fully is more than all these things. It is connection with the world in an integral way—a belonging that is vital, consequential, and immensely pleasurable.

In order to reclaim our self-esteem, we must discover and recover the missing pieces of our lives. As we fill in the holes, we become whole; we realize that we are holy. We are not sick, bad, crazy, or stupid, as we may have been told. We are, in fact, blessed.

Find Your Source

*"The child is an almost universal symbol for
the soul's transformation. The child is whole,
not yet divided.... When we would heal the mind...
we ask this child to speak to us."*

—Susan Griffin

Invisible and unknown to the larva, a miraculous design deep within is developing. Mysteriously guided to shed layer after layer of its smaller self, it is directed to participate in the miracle of transformation. The butterfly within—acting as a guardian angel or spirit guide—shows the way.

In reclaiming our self esteem, we connect more deeply and honestly with who we really are—with our True Self. In filling in the holes, we connect our adult-self back to our child-self, and we connect our individual-self to all of humanity.

For high self-esteem, we must also dive deep and feed the spirit—the life principle and animating force within our selves—and reclaim our spirituality. In connecting with the mystical depths of our being, we tap into our roots, our center, our soul, our core, and experience ourselves in a larger way—in relationship to the universe. This spiritual dimension can provide a solid anchor of love, value, and worth, like for the child who said, "I know I'm somebody 'cause God don't make no junk."

Exercises:

- Spend quiet time each day. Meditation, prayer, deep relaxation and solitude can help to connect us with our inner source, our place in the world, and the sacredness of all life.

- Develop a spiritual practice that keeps you on the path every day, one day at a time. It may be a traditionally religious one, such as reading from the Old or New Testament, or praying before meals or at bedtime. Or you might engage in physical meditation such as t'ai chi or a long walk in nature. Many very simple activities can feed your soul, from cooking to painting, from gardening to writing, or simply reaching out to others. Joseph Campbell once commented: "All of life is a meditation, most of it unintentional."

- Look for the miracles. Buddhist monk Thich Nhat Hanh wrote, "Every day we are engaged in a miracle that we don't even recognize: a blue sky, white clouds, green leaves, the black inquisitive eyes of a child—our own two eyes. All is a miracle."

Who's Pulling Your Strings?

*"To be no one but yourself in a world which is
doing its best to make you just like
everybody else means to fight the greatest
battle there is or ever will be."*

—e. e. cummings

Little children look up to the adults in their lives to tell them what to do. The grown-ups seem to know it all, have it all together, have all the power. In healthy families, children discover (through being listened to) that what they have to say is important, and that their experiences and ideas (and they themselves) have worth. They are encouraged to think for themselves, express opinions, and make decisions for themselves. Parents support them in standing on their own two feet and doing what they think is right. Trusting and gaining confidence in themselves, they develop an inner locus of control.

When this process does not occur in children—when their parents do not empower them—as adults they will continue to look to others to take charge of them, take care of them, and tell them what to do. They avoid personal responsibility for their lives. They trust others more than they trust themselves. And when something goes wrong, they can, of course, blame somebody else.

Such persons with an external locus of control believe that they are not the cause, but the effect of circumstances, other persons' actions, their past, their emotions, and so on. These persons believe that no matter where they go, someone will control them. They have given their personal power to others, and they feel powerless.

Their self-talk is cluttered with "should's," "have to's," and "supposed to's," and they are confused about what they themselves want. Lacking an internal guidance center, they are vulnerable to manipulation and exploitation from every front. Feeling like victims, out of control of their lives, and worried about what the neighbors think, they suffer from powerlessness and low self-esteem.

Locus of control refers to the source of power and control in an individual's life. We start life with an external locus of control and, hopefully, internalize that power in early adulthood. If not, it's not too late! Cut those labels off your mattresses! The road from an external to an internal locus of control is the road to empowerment and self-determination.

Exercises:

- List five things you have to do after you put this book down. Start each sentence with "I have to...," "I ought to...," "I must...," or "I should...." Give yourself a few minutes to do this. Then, rewrite this same list starting every sentence with "I choose to...." Notice the difference. Which list is more likely to get done? People frequently report feeling out of control, burdened, and resistant with the first (external locus of control) list, and lighter and empowered with the second (inner locus of control) list.

- Listen for the *should's, supposed to's, have to's,* and *musts.* Red flag them. They can keep you unconsciously following old, out- dated programming. When you next hear a "should," stop. "Thou shalt not should upon thyself!" Then ask yourself what you *want* to do.

- Simplify your life. Americans own 400 percent more posses- sions now than in the 1940s. Every aspect—acquisition, main- tenance, storage, disposal—takes time and energy and keeps you externally focused. Is this how you want to spend your time, your life?

- Turn off the television. Create spaces of silence so you can tune in to what you want. Go for long walks. Learn to listen to your intuition, that small voice within. Tune in to inner listening— your divine guidance system. It will help you to distinguish what you really want from what you have been talked into.

- Own your own self. You have not been given anyone else's self to own, just your own self. Others are in charge of their selves, not your self. You are ultimately in charge of your actions and their consequences, and your life. You can never be separated from your self. Acknowledge, embrace, and act from this truth and take full possession of your life.

- Reclaim your power. You are under the control of a single brain, the brain that is in your head and nobody else's. Others have no power over you unless you grant them that power. Even if you do give your power to others, you do so only moment by moment. Any power that you may have given away is forever yours to reclaim.

- Inhabit your body. Listen to it. Learn to trust it. It is the source of deep wisdom and great pleasure. Embrace it. Take good care of it. Resolve to be your own best and most enduring friend, physically as well as mentally and spiritually.

Let Go of Perfectionism

"The only way you can describe a human being
truly is by describing his [or her] imperfections.
The perfect human being is uninteresting . . .
it is the imperfections of life that are lovable."

—Joseph Campbell

Back when I was a caterpillar, I worked very, very hard to be perfect. If I was perfect, I reasoned, then I would be "okay." In a flash of insight, I saw this as a mathematical equation: To Be Perfect = To Be Okay. Having studied algebra in high school, however, I knew that something was very wrong here. Slowly I started to identify the errors in my thinking. I began to dismantle that complex set of beliefs and behaviors, and I'm now enjoying life more as a "recovering perfectionist."

It's not easy being perfect when you're only human! Perfectionists always look for something wrong, find it, then are shocked and angry about it. They exhibit the following characteristics:

- Their impossible expectations constrict and inhibit their expression, stifle their creativity, and set them up for failure. They are constantly frustrated, disappointed, and angry.

- No matter how successful they are, they are never satisfied, they never appreciate their achievements or give themselves a pat on the back.
- They never feel "good enough."
- They are rigid and controlling of themselves—and others.
- They don't try, don't start, procrastinate, or don't finish projects.
- Mistakes, to perfectionists, are proof of total failure; they can devastate self-esteem.
- They are judgmental and critical of themselves and of everyone else.
- They always focus on what is wrong—the shortcomings, flaws, and imperfections—and miss all the things that are "right."
- They have difficulty with decisions because they're trying to make a "perfect" decision.
- Entangled in trivia, they can't see the big picture. They usually end up doing all the work themselves because no one else can do it "just right."
- Either-or thinking is common; as one women learned from her mother, "You are perfect or you are nothing." Perfectionists don't know how much room there really is between "perfect" and "total failure."
- Focusing on appearances, they miss the rich, internal dimensions of life. Instead of just allowing her feelings when her husband died, one woman ran out and bought several etiquette books on the subject so that she could grieve "perfectly."

Perfectionism is the world's greatest con game. It's a concept that doesn't fit reality. The second law of thermodynamics predicts that everything dissolves into chaos eventually. Perfectionism, therefore, is a losing battle. There are more important battles to fight. Perfectionism robs us of satisfaction, of joy, of self-esteem. These exercises can help you begin to release its stranglehold.

Exercises:

- Reorder your priorities. Imagine reviewing your life from your deathbed. What is most important to you? In those areas, go for excellence. Be fantastic! Be magnificent! In other areas, give yourself permission to be "good enough."

- Mistakes are teachers. It is your privilege as a human being to make mistakes—and your challenge to learn from them, and not repeat them. A mistake, after all, is just one way that doesn't work. Find other ways that *do* work. A wise person once remarked, "I'm failing my way to success." Learn the judgment skills and wisdom each mistake offers you. Then talk about and laugh at your bloopers.

- Stop the stinkin' thinkin' that says "I'm not good enough." Because you really are good enough! Not perfect, but good enough. Repeat this affirmation: "I, _____, *am* good enough." Try looking at yourself in the mirror when you say it. Say it as though you mean it about fifteen times each day, until you believe it, until you become it. Talk back to your negative self-talk.

- Post reminders. Once, feeling overwhelmed by the clutter of my home, I painted a sign that said, "Nothing's perfect, but it's all okay." It helped me name the source of my distress and gain some objectivity. You might post this reminder, or another that seems to fit, such as, "I'm not perfect, but I *am* okay." Repeat these affirmations for at least twenty-one days.

- Be gentle with yourself. Perfectionists are rigid and controlling and are their own worst enemy. But you can't fly with such a heavy load on your shoulders and on your heart. Let it go. Take a deep breath. Be more flexible. Loosen up and lighten up.

- Do something you wouldn't normally do. Stretch your limits. Take a risk. Forget trying to be perfect. Just get better every day.

- Let more fun, joy, silliness, and spontaneity come into your life. Go to a park. Swing. Go down the slide. Roll down a hill. Dance wildly. Make a fool of yourself! Then laugh at it all. Laughter dissolves rigidity and heals the soul.

Turn-About Statements

"Argue for your limitations, and they are yours!"

—Richard Bach

Life is pretty simple for caterpillars. Their main concerns are to eat and avoid being eaten. As they put one foot in front of the other, the miracle of metamorphosis works silently through them, preparing to take them to new heights.

Like the lowly caterpillars, we are part of a larger plan. Within us all lies the potential for miracles waiting to happen. As humans with free will, however, we can resist, sabotage, and abort our own trans-formations. One way we do that is with our language.

Words can guide, support, and direct us along the path to greatness. Or they can trip us up and drag us down. A wise person once said, it's easier to ride the horse in the direction it is going. We can enjoy the exciting ride towards the unfolding miracles in our lives, or we can fight against our true nature and make ourselves miserable.

Words have tremendous power. They move us forward or hold us back. They lift us up or bring us down. And what we say to ourselves repeatedly will inevitably become reality.

Exercises:

- Listen carefully to your words. Watch especially for these phrases:

    "That's the way I am ... (a complainer, for example)."

    "I can't help it if I'm ... (a loser ... in debt ...)."

    "I'm the kind of person who ...."

- Instead use turn-about statements:

    "In the past I ... (was a complainer), but now ... (I'm learning to ask for what I want)."

    "I used to ..., but now I'm ...."

- If you feel you have made a serious mistake, say, "That's not like me!" Then lift yourself back on course to being the person you want to be (and really are)—worthwhile, competent, capable, and getting better every day.

Appreciate Your Wins

"People with the Win mentality don't necessarily want someone else to lose. That's irrelevant. What matters is that they get what they want."

—Stephen R. Covey

In our win-lose society, most people spend a lot of time feeling like losers. Trained to look for shortcomings, we can easily overlook our accomplishments, then punish ourselves for failings, both real and imagined. The word "win" has had too narrow a definition. We need to expand the meaning of winning, of success. Every success, achievement, and accomplishment is a win. Every task crossed off your To-Do List is a win. Every time you show up at a support group is a win. Some days, getting out of bed is a win. A fruitful phone conversation, a sunrise run, a sincere compliment, a garage sale find, being early to a meeting—you are winning all the time!

Exercises:

- Write down ten wins of the last day. Then, some self-appreciation is in order: a pat on the back or a hug would be good. This is a great exercise with which to end each day. You'll be surprised at its effect on your self-esteem.

- When you need recognition, give it to yourself, or ask for it from others. Instead of complaining, for example, about how hard you work and how ungrateful everyone is, try saying, "I worked very hard today and would like...(some applause, flowers, hugs, or pats on the back)."

- Notice how you keep improving. Appreciate and celebrate your progress.
- Look also for others' successes and wins. Acknowledge them. Express your gratitude. Treat them as winners.

When you have a sense of your own worth, you realize that one person's success does not have to be at another's expense. You understand that you don't need to put others down or make them wrong, in order to feel up. When you seek solutions that are mutually satisfying and beneficial to all involved parties, you move from a "win-lose" to a "win-win" mode of operating your life.

Back-Sliding

"Success is getting up one more time
than you fall down."

—Julie Bowden

One day while driving down the freeway to visit my aging mother, I suddenly started feeling like an ugly, inadequate, bad little girl and forgot the capable, good woman that I had been when I got in the car. I observed this reverse metamorphosis with interest, musing how a beautiful butterfly had just given way to the caterpillar of times past. Identifying this "age regression" gave me the distance and objectivity I needed to take some action and lift myself out of the drama of the moment.

Perhaps something like this has happened to you. Perhaps you, a grown-up adult, have returned to your childhood home, knocked at the door, and suddenly became a five-year-old kid again with five-year-old feelings. Sometimes it can feel as though you take two steps forward, and one back. As soon as you notice this, you can stop it and return to the wisdom which your years have since given you.

Exercises:

- Watch out for age regressions. Notice when you back-slide into old caterpillar ways. Take your inner child by the hand, listen to it, comfort it, protect it. Find out what's going on. Then return to the present with deeper insight and the strength you need to deal with the situation.

- Enhance your life with awareness. Keep examining the mental baggage that you carry with you, and select the course of action that will lift you out of tough situations.

Protect Your Self-Esteem

"Why do I so frequently need to protect myself
from those who say they love me?"

—Ashleigh Brilliant

As a young teacher fascinated by nature and metamorphosis, I took two tomato worms (Sphinx moth caterpillars) from my garden and put them in a clean waste basket in my kitchen. Daily I fed them fresh tomato plant leaves, and was amazed that I could hear them chew! One got bigger and bigger; the other didn't. One day, I discovered several long and narrow white objects projecting from the back of the smaller one. Doing some research, I learned that a certain wasp lays her eggs inside the defenseless tomato worm. The wasp larvae live and grow there until they emerge to continue their own life cycle.

All living things face life and death challenges. During the course of evolution, amazing protection strategies have developed. Defenses are crucial for survival, individually, and as a species. To illustrate, monarch butterfly larvae eat only the milkweed plant; toxins in this plant stay in the creature's body from the caterpillar stage to the butterfly. When a predator eats a monarch, it becomes sick and quickly learns to avoid them in the future. The viceroy butterfly also benefits—simply because it looks very much like the monarch, and predators avoid eating them as well.

We humans also need strategies for protecting ourselves—physically and emotionally (and in other ways as well). We need to know how to keep others from harming us. Once we accept responsibility for our self-esteem, we need to learn skills for protecting it when it's under attack. We need to know how to keep put-downs, criticism, prejudice, and humiliation from damaging our sense of self-worth.

Without such skills, people may turn to food for comfort, shopping for distraction, drugs and alcohol for relief, or tears for release.

Remember a time when you felt good about yourself and someone tossed an insult your way; chances are, you probably let it go right past thinking that it couldn't possibly be for you. Now, think of a time when your self-esteem was sagging and someone gave you a compliment. Did you find yourself looking between the lines for what they *really* meant? One woman attending my presentation reported that a friend complimented her on her sweater; to herself she said, "She probably likes it because it covers my fat." When you keep your self-esteem high, most of the pollution of negativity will roll off you. When you don't, it will find its way in regardless what is said to you.

Exercises:

Today, watch for barbs and arrows. Notice how you react and respond to them. Then notice when and how you get hooked. Expand your bag of tricks with some of these strategies:

- Confront. Many people hurt others; yet they may not realize it if we grin and bear it and don't let them know that it hurts. The next time that happens say, "Ouch!" "I don't like that," or "Stop that."

- Withdraw. At times it can save your life. But don't overuse it, because your world can get smaller and smaller.

- Talk with a friend. You can rebalance your mind and release the pain by discussing the situation.

- Inquire. "What did you mean by that?" puts the responsibility back on them. Talking it over can clear up miscommunication.

- Disagree. What they say is just their opinion. You know yourself better than they do. Give more importance to what you think and less to what *they* think.

- Don't take it personally. Perhaps they were having a bad day. Or maybe they were just careless. Try to figure out what's underneath the insult.

- Consider the source. Some people are toxic. They wallow in negativity. If you are near them, realize that that's how *they* are; it has nothing to do with the fine person *you* are.

- Sift through. Perhaps there is some truth in what they are saying, but they lack the skills and sensitivity to present it to you inoffensively. Is there a nugget of helpful information you can find in their comment?

- Positive self-talk. Try this affirmation: "No matter what you say or do to me, I am a worthwhile person." Repeat it silently to yourself or say it out loud.

Like all other skills, these take practice. You don't have to put up with put-downs. Protect your self-esteem with these and your own strategies and create more positive energy in this world.

Embrace the Darkness

"The depth of nothingness is directly related to
the experience of everythingness....
We learn we are cosmic beings not only in our
joy and ecstasy but also in our pain and sorrow."

—Matthew Fox

What did you learn to do with the pain and discomfort in your life? Most people were taught to deny it, to distract themselves, and/or to drug themselves. At times, everyone uses such strategies of avoidance to provide a time for regrouping, or a brief vacation. The danger lies when denial, distraction, and drugs become a way to avoid dealing with life. When you avoid, you do nothing, and nothing changes except, perhaps, your perceptions (which are probably inaccurate).

We have been taught to avoid, deny, and run from the negative. Yet there can be amazing richness hidden within and beneath the sadness, the grief, the pain, the anger. "The depths of our being are not all sunlit," writes Starhawk; "to see clearly, we must be willing to dive into the dark, inner abyss and acknowledge the creatures we may find there."

Many years ago, when my transformation was just getting under-way, I decided to take a harder look at myself than I ever had before. I decided to get to the bottom of my lack of self-worth, and to find out what was *really* wrong with me. Suspecting something awful, I scheduled personal time for a "monster hunt," and asked a friend to be on call just in case I found one! The day came and I dared lift the veil. I looked in all the nooks and searched in all the crannies of my being, but much to my relief, couldn't find anything *nearly* as awful as I had suspected. My fears and doubts turned out to be somehow connected to my better qualities. With that piece of work completed, I turned to the light. Walking towards the sun, my shadow walks closely behind me, but doesn't tackle or scare me.

Someone wise once said that most people are running from something that isn't chasing them. If we stop running and confront our demons, they lose their dreaded power over us. We become empow-ered, learn something new, and become something new.

Dodging pain takes more energy than facing it. When we avoid pain, we hold on to it, and it becomes chronic. As long as we keep avoiding, we can remain stuck in feelings of helplessness and numb-ness. We can cut ourselves off from the compassion of others, and can interrupt the ongoing process of healing. Sharing pain allows an opening for giving and receiving support, and for bonding.

Exercises:

- Learn to be more comfortable with discomfort. Pay attention to the tension.

- Listen to the pain. Have the courage to sit with it, look at it, embrace it, befriend it. Learn from it. Share it. Then let it go.

- Trust the empty spaces and silences. Play with the nothingness. Trust the process. If you get scared, call a friend or a counselor.

- Spend time writing in a journal. If you can't find the words, draw or paint or shape your feelings into a tangible form. Watch for the creativity that springs from the pain.

Set Goals and Go for Them!

"If you follow your bliss, you put yourself on
a kind of track that has been there the whole while,
waiting for you, and the life you ought to be
living is the one you are living."

—Joseph Campbell

Caterpillars don't think about goal setting. They just munch their way toward becoming a butterfly without worry, indecision, or anxiety. The writing is on the proverbial wall. If they survive, they cannot not become a butterfly or moth. There is no other option.

For humans, it's not quite that easy. For starters, we have innumerable options and free will to confuse us. Second, we often get overly involved with the struggle of the day, or dwelling on the past. We may simply continue repeating the old undesirable patterns because we missed learning lessons from the past. Third, people are frequently out of touch with their guidance system, or intuition, which is nudging them toward transformation. All of these things can make it difficult to imagine a future that is not a continuation of the past. But new ways of being are called for and goals can make them happen.

Goals are like maps that can help keep us on course in life or take us to uncharted heights. They are also like magnets. They can attract what we need for their accomplishment. Several times, for example, while writing this book, the perfect article or insight that I needed on the topic of the day suddenly and unexpectedly appeared. "The gods send thread," wrote Leif Smith, "for the web begun."

Exercises:

- Make a wish list. List the important areas of your life: family, friendships, career, finances, personal. Then, imagine what you would like for yourself in each category, and write them in. Finally, put a date on each item. A goal is a wish with a time line.

- Play with your list. You might cut up each list and prioritize it. Choose what you really want. Make a commitment to go for your most important goals.

- Make a treasure map for your highest ranked goals. Get poster board, magazines, scissors, and rubber cement, tape, or glue. Set aside at least twenty minutes for this project. Cut and paste pictures and words that symbolize each goal very clearly: what it will look like when you get there, how you will feel when you've achieved it, and the date by which it will be completed. Put this treasure map where you will see it frequently to remind you of your goal.

- Visualize. As Richard Bach said it, "To bring anything into your life, imagine that it is already there." A friend of mine visualizes a long, tightly stretched rubber band pulling her towards her goals.

- "Chunk it down." Divide the goal or project into bite-size, manageable pieces. Encourage and support each increment of success. Then congratulate yourself for every small achievement: "Good job!" "I'm proud of you." "Hooray!"

- Every day do one thing to move you closer to those goals. Get the momentum going, and don't lose it. If you get off track, lift yourself back up and continue.

In short: Live purposefully. Formulate goals. Make an action plan. Monitor your behavior to keep on track. Pay attention to outcome. And of course, always celebrate your successes! You've earned them!

PART III

WINGS OF SELF-ESTEEM

The Transformation
Is Complete

"What the caterpillar calls the end of the world,
the master calls a butterfly."
—Richard Bach

WHAT IS RECOVERY and how do you know you're there? Recovering from psychic trauma, addiction, or a lost sense of worth is different from recovering from an accident or illness, but similar in an important way. When a cold is gone, you can get out of bed, eat, breathe, and exercise again. When you recover from a flu, food tastes better, the air smells fresher, as if you can appreciate for the first time the good health you used to take for granted. Healing is a natural process. Human life has a built-in propensity for growing toward health and wholeness in body, mind, and spirit.

When you have had your self-esteem damaged and lived as a caterpillar, you may not remember what "normal"—or healthy—feels like. But you will notice your life getting better. A recovering addict will begin to notice all the good things in life that had previously been lost to him or her. A recovering alcoholic friend of mine, for instance, notices that he no longer feels terrible on Sunday mornings because he doesn't get drunk on Saturday nights anymore. When you can feel the difference in your life, you know the effort to give up unhealthy behaviors has been worth it.

Our call is to heal the wounds of childhood and adolescence, and to incorporate the wisdom and the passion into the next stage of development. Our call is to be full participants in life and to take our place in the turbulent, exciting, and evolving world.

Part Three is about what happens after the cocoon stage. It's about outcomes. It's about rewards. But it's mostly about butterflies. It will not tell you to change jobs, have a baby, or take that trip. You know what to do. You need to take it from here. You're flying now.

10

EMERGING

"You can fly, but that cocoon has got to go."

—Anonymous

ONE SPRING morning, Zorba the Greek discovered a cocoon just as the butterfly was making a hole and trying to get out. Impatient with the slowness of the event, he breathed on it to give it some warmth. Then, faster than life, a miracle happened. The butterfly emerged!

With a trembling body, the creature tried to unfold its crumpled wings. Again Zorba breathed on it to warm it. To his horror he realized that, in trying to help, he had forced the metamorphosis before its time. The butterfly struggled desperately for a few moments, then died in the palm of his hand. Although Zorba had meant to help the butterfly, his good intentions brought its doom.

"I do believe," he said, "that little body is the greatest weight I have on my conscience. For I realize today that it is a mortal sin to violate the greatest laws of nature. We should not hurry, we should not be impatient, but we should confidently obey the eternal rhythm."

Sometimes it's hard to be patient with the timetable of life. We, too, may be tempted to find a bypass or a shortcut. Growth and development, however, for bumblebees, butterflies, and humans alike, have their own timetable. We can stimulate and enhance growth, but we cannot force it.

When we observe and study nature, we learn a great deal about process. Seeds may lie dormant for a long time until the sun shines, the rain falls, or a rock is moved out of the way. When conditions are right, they grow, blossom, and bear fruit. Like lilies and wildflowers, we, too, bloom in our own time, in our own way. When will it happen? Will it happen all at once?

How does a daffodil or a rose know that it's time to blossom? When does the butterfly know it's time to emerge, to take that final step and complete its transformation? How do we know when it's time for us? What message or messenger will signal the metamorphosis?

Gradually or suddenly, there comes a new uneasiness and the cocoon walls that have kept us safe for so long begin to chafe ever so slightly. A hole appears in the hard shell of our cocoon, and a stream of light enters the dark sanctuary. Then there is a difference in the air. The climate is warmer. The smells of a new, yet familiar world, and the songs of the birds stir a desire to join in. A surge of excitement pulses through our veins with the promise of new life. The moment of birth, of new beginnings has finally arrived.

Perched on that threshold, however, we can undermine the metamorphosis in a variety of ways. We can try to force the process, as Zorba did. Or we can try to resist it—like the caterpillar who looked up at a butterfly and said, "You'll never get me up in one of those things!" Instead of letting go, trusting, and transforming, we can get in our own way, trip ourselves up, and sabotage our growth. "That's the way I am; always have been, always will be." We can convince ourselves that we're just caterpillars with no potential greater than munching and getting fat. We can continue the discouraging and disempowering opinions, judgments, and beliefs—emphatically displaying the evidence we've collected and held on to over the years to prove that we're right. We can cling to the habitual, insecure thoughts and behaviors that create fear, stress, and anxiety, and which hold us back. And we can anesthetize ourselves through denial, distraction, and drugs and ignore the stirrings to live more fully.

On the other hand, when we feel the quickening, we can say "Yes!" to the invitation. And, like the butterfly, in order to fly we shed that which has weighed heavily on our hearts and souls. We can take ourselves more lightly.

It may take days. It may take months. It may take years before a human butterfly is ready to emerge. Do it at your own pace. Be aware that this transition period can be the hardest and most vulnerable time in your life. Be gentle with yourself. Keep in good company, letting no one call you out too soon, letting no one hold you back. Your long history as a caterpillar has been preparing you to become one tremendously beautiful butterfly.

If a creepy crawling caterpillar can become a fabulous butterfly with gossamer wings, anything is possible for us! With our minds, intuition, hearts, and free will, we can do almost anything. We can transcend our old self and see the world with new eyes. We can achieve the miraculous.

> *"Our primary responsibility, our destiny is to stand up and say and be who we are! There are no models, no blueprints. No one can show us. We are commissioned to this creativity by the universe. This is our greatest contribution to this, our moment in the unfolding story—to be who we are fully."*
>
> —Brian Swimme

11

FLYING

"The winds will blow their own freshness into you,
and the storms their energy, while cares will
drop off like autumn leaves."
—John Muir

THE DIFFERENCE between a caterpillar and a butterfly is vast. It's as profound a difference as between counting on your fingers and being able to multiply with your imagination. Between traveling by Conestoga wagon and taking an airplane. And transformation for caterpillars and humans alike is a natural life phenomenon.

A caterpillar need depend only on gravity. A butterfly's life requires that it trust the energy of the winds. All its choices are contingent on the weather. Weather can be its greatest friend or its biggest challenge. Like the weather, the movements and patterns of our interactions and emotions also affect our lives. We have little control over outside events, yet must somehow manage to stay on our course and soar to our heights.

There are an infinite number of variables to life—so many moments in which unknown things can happen, so many levels on which we experience things. No two days, two people, two snowflakes are the same. There are so many forces acting upon us, and within us. In many ways, life on planet earth is fundamentally unpredictable, and this unpredictability can be frightening.

We may be flying along on a lovely sunny day, when suddenly, a crack of thunder and a gust of wind come, and throw us off balance. The vastness of the universe can shake us to the core. We may slip into insecurity, and be tempted to fall back into negative habits or old addictions. Yet we have wings. We go on.

There are times to fly, and times to rest. And as sure as we breathe and blink, our hearts and minds are constantly in a state of change. We must constantly reevaluate our priorities and reaffirm our commitments. A recovering alcoholic, for example, sober for forty years, must choose every day to remain sober. Recovery is the process of living life deliberately, a never-ending process. In other words, butterflies have to keep flapping their wings, making choices every day. It's a lot of work.

Marilyn Ferguson states that "Once the journey has begun in earnest, there is nothing that can dissuade." An object in motion tends to stay in motion. Once you have deliberately walked a path long enough to let it transform you, it is part of you.

The rhythm of the universe is full of surprises. Periodically, the chaos of the universe will pull you away from your path, and that's okay. We are all affected by the patterns of a complex and multi-leveled system—Life. From the butterflies we can learn how to let these gusts come and go.

Monarch butterflies have yet another lesson for us humans. Since these delicate creatures cannot survive extended periods of freezing temperature in any stage of their life cycle, they migrate. Those living west of the Rocky Mountains fly to the California coast; those east of the Rockies migrate to Mexico. One monarch that was marked in Toronto appeared in Mexico; it had flown 1,870 miles to reach its destination!

Between 50,000 and 200,000 of this species spend their winters in a park in Santa Cruz, California. Instinct guides them to cluster in the tall eucalyptus trees. The massive clumps of wiggling orange velvet wings grow so heavy they bend the tree's branches toward the ground.

Combining their weight keeps the butterflies from being dislodged by the rain and wind. Clinging together keeps them alive. Human observers of this awesome sight get a very clear under-standing of the importance of community. If a butterfly is separated from the cluster and the temperature is too cold for it to fly, it ends up on the ground vulnerable to the elements and to predators.

We all value independence and freedom in this country. Yet for some of us, the need for independence has become so strong that we start to believe there is something wrong with needing other people. Yet without each other we are isolated and immensely vulnerable. The myth of separateness has led to protectiveness, loneliness, and a profound sense of disconnectedness and isolation. Yet we are all connected. We are, in fact, all part of one very large, very diverse, and very human family. We are actually more alike than different. And like the monarchs, at times we must cluster for our very survival.

On their migratory routes, monarchs will choose to stop and rest in the exact same tree their parents flocked to over the years for countless generations. Without ever having stopped there themselves, their instincts, or genetic memories, lead them to the places where they belong. Like them, we need to rely on ourselves, on our experience, our memories, our deepest intuition to divine the places where we fit in—families, places, cultures. Without these things, we are homeless. Connections and traditions help us to know who we are.

The paradigm shift from crawling to flying allows a new relationship with the earth—another dimension in which to experience and enjoy the world. When we transform, we open ourselves to aspects of living that may never have occurred to us. Our senses awaken, our hearts and minds open, and our imagination takes us to new places.

Old compulsions and addictions are released by the new pleasure we discover in life, and our ability to trust the flow of our emotions. We discover the natural highs that have always been available on earth: the simplicity of lying on the grass in the sunshine, taking a long hike in a beautiful place, riding a horse at a full gallop, dancing a Viennese waltz, finding the answer to a long-sought question, connecting with cherished friends, and shouting for the joy of it.

With our new eyes we can see that the joys and sorrows, the pits and peaks, the love and the pain are places that the winds of life take us if we let them. A caterpillar cannot know these things until it is transformed. This is true, also, for humans. Transformation introduces infinite possibilities for joy, adventure, love, and delight which bring lightness and continual renewal to the soul. Life itself becomes its own reward.

"There are only two ways to live your life.
One is as though nothing is a miracle.
The other is as though everything is a miracle."

—Albert Einstein

12

The Sky's the Limit!

"A butterfly flaps its wings in the Amazon,
and it rains over Central Park."

—Anonymous

A CATERPILLAR IS an eating machine whose purpose is to consume the bulk and roughage of green leaves, and process it into energy so that it can eat more and grow fatter. A butterfly, on the other hand, sips the rarified nectar of flowers, the plant's essence, through its intricate and delicate proboscis. The concentrated sugars and proteins of the ambrosia give it the energy to fly.

Likewise, an enlightened person chooses his or her thoughts and attitudes carefully, to avoid being burdened with negativity. Lightness is a prerequisite for flying. Lightness of heart is a sign that we are on our way. We can use the fullness of our passions and yearnings and skills to expand our magnificent wings and fly.

For a butterfly the weather is a metaphor for the motions of the universe. As individuals, we each have to negotiate under conditions that may have been set up in our childhood—our "personal weather patterns." These unique patterns affect us, yet we also have power to affect them. It is only we who can fly in them; only we who can change them. The effects of our actions are often beyond our comprehension. Yet when we use our tools for flying—our wings and our wisdom—our most subtle efforts can have far-reaching effects.

The Butterfly Effect, discovered by meteorologist Edward Lorenz, demonstrates how a slight alteration in the initial condition of a weather system will affect major alterations in the behavior of the system. In other words, we are all participating in interconnected systems which we influence beyond our awareness. We don't know what effects we will ultimately have on the world when we greet strangers on the sidewalk, spend a few dollars at the market, write a letter. But that embrace we give our child today may translate to a hundred of our great-great-great grandchildren hugging their children two hundred years from now. Every good thing is forever.

We all have our own personal stories of healing, heroism, and overcoming obstacles in our lives. And we are all enveloped in a larger, unfolding tapestry that stretches to the horizons of our imagination. Our own personal evolution may, in fact, be just a small part of the larger process of human evolution.

Our personal struggles during our caterpillar phase resulted from the problems and dysfunction of society over the years. During our history of conquest and survival on this planet, we humans have been split into mind, body, spirit, and emotion; these facets of our being have sometimes been put to war with the others. We have been separated from nature and lost our deep connections with family and community. We have tried to feel better about ourselves by being better than others. Comparing and competing have driven wedges between people who belong together.

Those who have had power have over-used and abused it, dominating others, creating violence, war, and victimization of innocents. Underlying attitudes of negativity and pessimism have culminated in our low self-esteem, helplessness, and despair.

Our individual revelations and collective struggles have brought about personal and cultural metamorphoses, moving us beyond that old paradigm. Once we become butterflies, everything looks different from our new vantage point. We are now participating in the creation of a new paradigm for humankind. Says Alvin Toffler, "We are the final generation of an old civilization and the first generation of a new one."

In the new world view we realize that we're not estranged from or separate from nature, but are one with her and depend upon her for our very survival. We come to value compassion, balance, power-sharing, peace, diversity, cooperation, and integrity in our personal and social interactions. Mutual respect, empowerment, and win-win thinking transform our relationships into partnerships. As we discover the deep pleasures of healthy relations, our families and communities become more harmonious as well. Our attitude becomes optimistic, we expect the best and look for new possibilities and opportunities. This expanding consciousness brings us a sense of meaning and purpose, hope and high self-esteem.

This is a glimpse of where we are going. This is what we are becoming. We are reconnecting and reclaiming our missing pieces and becoming whole and holy.

*　*　*

Everything begins with our vision—how we choose to view the world. When we look with fresh eyes, we can see that disintegration precedes integration, breakdown precedes breakthrough, endings precede new beginnings, death precedes rebirth, and winter precedes springtime. And when we stretch our wings, we know that we are part of the undying dance.

"We can never be born enough. We are
human beings for whom birth is a supremely
welcome mystery, the mystery of growing...,
the mystery which happens only and whenever
we are faithful to ourselves."

—e. e. cummings

EPILOGUE

TRANSFORMATION can start with a whisper or a shout, with a phone call or a flash of insight. Life calls us forth every day with new surprises, gifts, and opportunities for change. Some changes are small, others huge, and they can all eventually add up to transformation beyond our wildest dreams.

The seeds of my own transformation were planted when I began to raise my children in a healthier way than I had been raised. The seedlings then began to blossom when my marriage ended. What looked to me like the end of the world was, in fact, the beginning of life in a new world. Until that time, my identity had coincided with my roles. When people asked me who I was, I'd answer, "I'm a housewife" or, "I'm just a mom." Those many years of being at home for my youngsters were the wellspring that led to writing my first book, *The Winning Family*. I never dreamt at that time that I was already doing my life's work and would someday be an author! I never imagined the challenges I would face and overcome.

I took that courageous and outrageous first step out of desperation—even though it looked crazy to others, even though I was told that I'd never make it on my own. My journey and growth began instantly and intensely. I did things I never thought I could do.

At age 38, I took my first classes in gymnastics, assertiveness, meditation, and belly dancing. With the help of a mechanic, I overhauled the engine of my car. I went trekking in the mountains of Nepal. And most importantly, I moved beyond my terror of speaking in public, which set me on the path of my life's work. I am now a professional speaker on behalf of growing healthy families.

Transformation does not make us into new people. Even when we can overcome the past, we still have our roots in it. I can now see that the pain of my childhood and the struggle with my marriage became the source of my passion for my life's work. It seems, in hindsight, that there was a plan for my life all along. Yet, munching along as a caterpillar, I could not see it. In fact, when I was 45 years old, I still didn't know what I wanted to be when I grew up!

Now, at this stage of my life, I am flying. From this vantage point, the pieces of my life fit together and somehow make sense. The long process has led me to my mission and purpose in life. I am on the right path—the path with heart. And in a deep way, it feels right and good.